Designing
and
Delivering
Modules

David Turner

© Oxford Centre for Staff and Learning Development 2002

Published by
THE OXFORD CENTRE FOR STAFF AND LEARNING DEVELOPMENT
Oxford Brookes University
Gipsy Lane
Headington
Oxford
OX3 0BP

Designing and Delivering Modules
ISBN 1 873576 67 6

British Library Cataloguing-in-Publication Data.
A catalogue record for this book is available from the British Library.

Designed and typeset in Palatino and Helvetica by
Meg Richardson (megrichardson@btconnect.com).

Printed in Great Britain by
Technique Studios Limited
www.techniquestudios.com

Printed on paper produced from sustainable forests.

Contents

PART 2   Delivering modules

Preface

This book has developed from drafts of part of Chapter 4, and of Chapters 5, 7 and 8, that Graham Gibbs was working on when he left Oxford Brookes University for the Open University. To it I have brought my own experience which has included teaching, leading a course team and a subject group, course planning, modular course administration and management, external assessment and membership of validation panels and of various working groups concerned with academic credit and assessment.

In practice that experience has involved amongst many other things: trying to deliver compulsory modules which many students regarded as 'too difficult' or irrelevant; teaching as part of a team for an interdisciplinary module; coping with bureaucratic approaches to accreditation when modular programmes tended to be looked down upon as inferior to conventional honours degrees; attending course review meetings and sharing the insights gained from one subject area, to help solve problems that were experienced in another; sitting on validation panels and recognising that details of delivery and organisational constraints are important; and taking opportunities to help free up some regulations that wrongly constrained teaching and learning, and to tighten others to improve standards and equity. Through working informally and formally with colleagues in other institutions I've realised just how important it is to have a user-friendly computer management system and institution-wide agreement and implementation of some deadlines and procedures if there is to be real student choice. I have attempted to bring together the experiences of many people as well as my own, to provide many ideas to try out and warnings about what needs to be avoided.

You may gather from this that I think modularity is a 'good thing' and that many of the criticisms one hears are blinkered or biased. But I do not believe that modularity comes without problems or a flip side, or that all criticisms are born of prejudice. Fortunately in the Brookes scheme there was in the past, a general desire amongst the subject leaders to improve the modular scheme. This was possible largely because it was set up with a staff forum, led by a chair or dean, where people listened to others' problems and recognised that consensus was the best basis if the scheme was to deliver the benefits that most wanted. Distinguishing *real* problems from entrenched attitudes or simple conflict with academic traditions, tackling them and if necessary changing the scheme rules, regulations or procedures is, in my view, the proper way forward. But I believe it will only work properly if *you* want to make it work and *you* may have to work hard to achieve that.

In the present environment in Higher Education with the Quality Assurance Agency (QAA) frequently introducing new practices and updating existing ones, it also seemed important to provide an overview of QAA practice – at least as it existed in summer 2001! Hopefully some of the ideas in this book will help you tackle your problems.

David Turner, April 2002

Acknowledgements

Many people have contributed to this book. I would like especially to thank Graham Gibbs for the basic ideas in Chapters 5 to 8, and the many people Graham worked with as a staff developer, who were the source of many of the practitioners' quotes. Ideas and experiences which I have taken from the published work of others has been acknowledged and copyright permission has been sought although a few authors have not been traced. Inevitably over the years through conferences, workshops, validations, reviews and many other ways, I must have heard things from people which have simply become part of my own knowledge and experience without any clear memory of where I first heard them. These could not be acknowledged and I have regarded them as 'in the public domain'. My apologies to anyone who feels their contribution should have been explicitly acknowledged.

I would, however, like to acknowledge the useful (and not quite endless) discussions about credit I have had over the years with colleagues in the Southern England Consortium for Credit Accumulation and Transfer (SEEC); the sharing of ideas on assessment and regulations with those in the Student Assessment and Classification Working Group (SACWG); with those in Brookes over validation, 'enterprise', skills development, and especially with those in the Undergraduate Modular Scheme Management Team about 'how to make modularity work'. I would also like to acknowledge the help and advice received from Annette Turner on the use of resource-based learning and the issue of accessibility and assistive technology in particular. Finally my thanks to Sandy Meredith for her help in turning my draft of what is now Chapters 2 to 4, into a readable discourse.

Introduction

It was in the early 1970s that *modular degrees* were started at what are now London Guildhall and Oxford Brookes Universities and the Open University began to develop its own unit-based awards. But modularity developed so fast that at the end of the 1980s, David Watson et al (1989) wrote:

> Modularity was perhaps the buzz word of secondary and higher education in the 1980s ... in its simplest sense, then, 'modularity' implies no more than the division of a course into separate elements, each presented to the student ... with separable aims, objectives and a self-contained assessment scheme.

They went on to distinguish modular schemes that 'have used the term to reflect a mere crude division of a more conventional scheme' from those that have been committed to additional *modular* principles of *credit accumulation, progressive assessment* and *responsibility and choice*.

Those developments have continued apace and it is now estimated that 95% of higher education institutions in the UK base their courses on credit-bearing units or modules (QAA,1999a). This growth has been supported by many books, articles, workshops and conferences concerned with the overall features of modular structure and administration. For this author 'modularity' now implies:

- the use of 'academic credit' as a useful currency for learners and programme planners;

- the use of 'outcomes' and their associated assessment as a proper basis for specifying learning;

- that schemes will allow students to study topics in combinations largely of their own choosing;

- that there will be transparency with regard to what goes on in modules and what results are achieved; and

- that learning is valued however it has been achieved.

Other ideas such as credit tariffs, credit transfer, accreditation of prior learning, award frameworks, and opportunities for student choice through optional modules, and through interdisciplinary and cross disciplinary awards, follow from them.

The core premise, though, is that it is possible to carve learning into chunks (modules), to invite learners to join in the learning and teaching activities associated with a chunk, and to enable them to demonstrate whether they have assimilated that learning. This book is about the process of carving up learning into chunks and providing mechanisms for supporting students as they try to absorb those chunks. It is written for academic staff who want to design and deliver modules that work.

The material in this book:

- identifies and analyses the main teaching, learning and assessment problems modules present and the main opportunities they offer;

- raises module design issues concerning learning outcomes, learning activities and module description formats and their relationship to standards; and

- examines practical examples of a wide range of strategies for tackling the most common problems and for making modules work.

Modular schemes

Modular schemes were introduced for a number of reasons:

- recognition of the importance of offering students choice;

- greater cost effectiveness when government funding per student was being reduced;

- easier 'central' control either at institution or at faculty level;

- more flexibility in coping with the consequences of a 'widening participation' admissions policy; and even

- the need for staff development.

We absorb most of what we know osmotically from newspapers, television, books, gossip.

Dawkins (1999)

Some of the by-products of modular schemes were also seen as desirable by many in higher education (HE) when compared with the linear courses they replaced. These include:

- improved transparency of what was actually done in a degree course;

2

- improved awareness by students as to how they were progressing and what was required of them;

- easier evaluation and consequent improvement of the components (modules);

- increased provision of multidisciplinary and interdisciplinary awards;

- easier development of new award programmes; and

- easier incorporation of intermediate awards offering alternative end points.

By the end of the 1990s, the provision of and participation in HE had changed so much that non-modular programmes were being required to be as thorough in their specification and as flexible in their admissions policy as modular programmes. Insofar as this is a good thing, because it means HE is more accountable to and more aware of its stakeholders, there are grounds for claiming that modularity has contributed to an improvement in HE.

Common criticisms of modular schemes

Some of the problems designers and teachers of individual modules face are different from problems arising from conventional courses. Unfortunately it is not uncommon for modular systems to have been imposed on institutions or departments for one reason or another, with inadequate motivation for staff involvement. Staff energy gets consumed by opposition to the imposition, instead of learning how to develop satisfactory programmes and design modules that fit well within the programme.

As late as 1990 when modular schemes had become popular, they were still being criticised as superficial 'pick and mix' courses. Sceptics still derided modular programmes as mere disconnected academic collections: 'It is nonsense to use listings of credit units as anything but the vaguest intimation of what degree courses are all about' (Goodlad, 1999). Such a criticism would be valid if all a modular scheme consisted of was such a listing. The same criticism might be made of a conventional course in which students were offered a list of options and no other information about those options. However, in a well-designed modular programme, detailed module specifications provide an abundance of information about what students are expected to learn. No surprise then that Goodlad's criticism was part of a broader attack on the idea that benchmark specifications expressed in terms of learning outcomes could lead to improved degree-level education.

Could it be that ... the stripping away of course offerings into the thin gruel of intellectually anaemic modules ... (leads to the lack of a) correlation between quality in research and quality in teaching...?

Staddon (2000)

Many of the so-called 'problems with modular schemes' are often identified by comparison with courses set in a bygone age when staff simply passed on their wisdom and knowledge to students who wanted a learning 'experience' more than a degree. Stephen Court (2002), writing in the Bulletin of the Association of University Teachers (AUT), states:

> Over the past 20 years the ratio of students to teaching staff in UK universities has doubled. The student:staff ratio (SSR) of 18:1 is now the same as the pupil:teacher ratio in schools... For staff, the rapid increase in workload has resulted in often excessive hours being worked and additional occupational stress. For students, the quality of the education they experience has been impaired by reduced contact time with staff, cramped teaching and research space, and often inadequate learning resources.

It is these resource pressures which have forced universities in general to decrease the staff contact with students and encouraged the development of modular schemes. The critics have, on the whole, naively claimed that modularity has caused the problems which it is in fact being used, at least in part, to overcome.

These issues have become more complex as a consequence of benchmarking and other items on the national 'standards' agenda. However, these differences should not be exaggerated; many of the problems characteristically attributed to modular courses are nothing to do with modularity per se but may be:

- the consequence of bizarre regulations imposed at the same time as modularisation, such as the imposition of standardised teaching patterns regardless of the needs of a subject or module;

- due to inadequate administrative systems, for example not knowing how many students you will have on your module; or

- features that have gone unnoticed before because course design was taken for granted and poorly evaluated, for example the claim that student workloads or grade distributions are more varied between modules now than they used to be between courses.

I have the greatest respect for the university ... but I must confess that I'm not entirely clear what it's for ... perhaps it is time to re-address one's educational priorities.

Bryson (1993)

Challenges for lecturers

There are, however, a range of problems encountered by lecturers that are characteristic of modules rather than of courses. These are associated primarily with:

- the duration and size of modules in terms of learning hours – modules tend to be completed in a shorter period than the parts of the courses they replaced;

- the diversity of students on modules – students on modules tend to come from a wider variety of academic backgrounds with less predictable knowledge, skills and interests and with less social cohesion;

- enrolment – modularity has increased average enrolment, especially in first-year introductory and service modules, and often produces apparently unpredictable enrolments;

- centralisation – modularisation often appears to be associated with the centralisation of a greater proportion of design decisions and regulations, leaving lecturers with less scope for solving problems within modules;

- preoccupation with modules – once all learning is deemed to take place within modules, and all funding is associated with enrolment on modules, other components of learning support, such as personal tutoring, may be neglected; and

- an emphasis on assessment – in most cases students need to pass those modules they 'take'; if there were no assessment in a particular module then most students would not bother to 'take' it.

Many of these grounds for complaint have been argued about in the past. Some of them will be addressed in this book but the points about centralisation and emphasis on assessment are effectively enshrined in standards developed by the QAA (Quality Assurance Agency): the National Qualifications Framework (NQF), programme specifications, benchmark statements and codes of practice. The next chapter is about these standards, and about national systems of credit designed to enhance student progression through the post-school educational system.

How to use this book

The book is designed to help the new lecturer, or the lecturer new to modules, to design and deliver effective modules to enhance student learning. It is divided into two sections: (1) design; (2) delivery. It is aimed at providing workable and useful ideas, not recipes, but it is intended to be pragmatic, working with the organisations and institutions that we have, rather than arguing for a different environment, approach, funding system, resources or whatever. To get the most out of this book, start by identifying your most urgent and important concern with regard to your module and go to the appropriate chapter or section. They do not need to be studied sequentially.

What you want to know	Where to find it	What is there
Design issues		
Where your module fits in relation to the national and institutional requirements	Chapter 2 & Appendices	Examples of national standards from the QAA; general aspects of modular schemes
How to comply with the rules and regulations for your module at the institutional level	Chapter 3	Advice about understanding and using rules and regulations
What the important elements of designing your module are	Chapter 4	How to use learning outcomes and specify teaching, learning and assessment to fit a programme specification
Delivery practices		
How to deliver your whole module when you have only a term or semester	Chapter 5	Ideas for getting going from the first session
How to cope with student diversity	Chapter 6	How to help students start from a common base and how to use diversity to enrich your teaching
How to mark work and provide useful feedback in the limited time you have	Chapter 7	How to use different assessment methods for different purposes and reduce the time involved in feedback
How to get feedback from students that helps you improve the module	Chapter 8	How to collect evaluation data in different ways and focus on specific issues

Module design – the national context

... public money is being wasted in the overly bureaucratic regulation of higher education ... More than £250 million is spent each year on quality assurance (UPDATE, 2001).

At the top of the hierarchy that sets standards for Higher Education (HE) stands the Quality Assurance Agency (QAA). Its National Qualification Framework (NQF) is expected to ensure that all HE awards in the UK have certain minimum requirements (QAA, 2001a). Four main 'purposes' are given for adopting this framework but from the point of view of the lecturer, the two most important are:

- to assist learners to identify potential progression routes, particularly in the context of lifelong learning; and

- to assist higher education institutions, their external examiners and the Agency's reviewers, by providing important points of reference for setting and assessing standards.

The terminology of the QAA framework and how the hierarchy works will be briefly explained in this chapter. If you are familiar with this material, you may wish to go straight to Chapter 3, which is about the local context in which your module fits.

Outcomes

Broadly speaking, the educational philosophy on which the QAA framework is based reflects an outcomes-based approach. An outcome is simply a result or consequence of an action or process; the outcome from a learning process is a learning outcome. Students who are successful in attaining awards are expected to have demonstrated achievement of specified learning outcomes. When designing modules, lecturers are expected to specify learning outcomes, and to adopt teaching and learning, and assessment methods that enable students to demonstrate achievement of them.

Qualification descriptors

These generic statements of the outcomes of study have two parts:

- a statement of outcomes a student should achieve for the award of the qualification; and

- a statement of the wider abilities a typical student could be expected to have developed.

Terminology and the QAA

The QAA has developed a series of statements about expected educational standards. The terms in this box are briefly described in this chapter, with examples provided in the appendices. For more on the QAA documents go to www.qaa.ac.uk.

outcomes	sets of statements about attainment of a student who holds a particular award
level	qualifications sharing similar outcomes
qualification descriptors	generic statements of the outcomes of study
benchmark statements	further guidance on expectations for particular subjects at Honours level
programme specifications	standard sets of information provided by institutions about their programmes
amount of learning	expressed in terms of study time or credit rating
threshold standards	statements about minimum standards of assessment to achieve awards
academic review	a process used to determine whether the intended outcomes for programmes are appropriate and achieved.

The statements specify what successful students (will) have demonstrated, what they will be able to do, and what qualities and transferable skills necessary for employment they will have – for example, 'an ability to deploy accurately established techniques of analysis and enquiry', the ability to 'critically evaluate arguments', and 'the learning ability needed to undertake further professional training'. Appendix 1 presents these descriptors for honours degrees, which are commonly regarded as the 'gold standard' of the UK HE system. According to QAA requirements, your 'curriculum and assessments have to provide all students with the opportunity to achieve, and to demonstrate achievement of the outcomes' (QAA, 2001a, p. 5). Note that general and specific skills are NOT addressed here but in subject benchmark statements and individual programme specifications *q.v.*

Benchmark statements

... a significant minority of staff are likely to resist an outcomes based approach.

Jackson (1998b, p. 138)

The development of subject benchmark standards was a key recommendation of the Dearing Report on Higher Education (NCIHE, 1997). Jackson (1998a) defines benchmarking as 'a collaborative learning process to facilitate the systematic comparison and evaluation of practice, process and performance to aid improvement and regulation' (p. 138). On this basis, as at summer 2001, the QAA is in the process of developing benchmark statements for programmes in 42 subjects. These benchmark statements have a common structure providing a great deal

Levels			
The NQF has five levels:			
1	Certificate	C level	Certificates of higher education
2	Intermediate	I level	Foundation degrees, ordinary (bachelors) degrees, diplomas of higher education and other higher diplomas
3	Honours	H level	Bachelors degrees with honours, graduate certificates and graduate diplomas
4	Masters	M level	Masters degrees, postgraduate certificates and postgraduate diplomas
5	Doctoral	D level	Doctorates

of detail about the expectations for degrees in particular subjects, including knowledge domains, skills, teaching and learning methods, assessment, and more. At the time of writing these were only available at the honours level, but they are being produced for other levels where there is significant taught provision in a subject.

When creating a programme specification (see below), the information in subject benchmark statements must be taken into account. Obviously these benchmarks will also impact upon the design of individual modules but there are considerable differences between subjects in the format, type of detail and terminology which are used, although they have similar components. Only by consulting your subject benchmark statement can you hope to work out the implications for your module. The 'knowledge' section of the draft psychology standards (QAA, 2001b), for example, specifies topic areas such as biological and cognitive psychology, and sub-areas such as pyschometrics. The 'skills' section in the draft physics standards (QAA, 2001c) specifies physics skills such as formulating and tackling problems, and transferable skills such as developing skills of independent investigation. The 'teaching, learning and assessment' section of the draft music standards (QAA, 2001d) specifies a substantial range of teaching and learning methods, from lectures to masterclasses, external placements, peer learning and so on. Comparisons of and extracts from these draft benchmark statements can be found in Appendix 2.

Programme specifications

Programme specifications too were one of the recommendations of the Dearing Report. They are based on the NQF and benchmark statements, but provide a much more specific account of the intended learning outcomes of a programme of study than these more general points of reference. According to the QAA Guidelines (2001, p. 3):

> Programme specifications should make explicit the intended outcomes in terms of knowledge, understanding, skills and other attributes. They should help students to understand the teaching and learning methods that enable the outcomes to be achieved; the assessment methods that enable achievement to be demonstrated; and the relationship of the programme and its study elements to the qualifications framework and to any subsequent professional qualification or career path.

Extracts from two examples of subject pathways and programme outcomes in the QAA Guidelines (2001) are presented in Appendix 3.

Programme specifications are produced within the institution. Your module has to play its part in preparing students to achieve the outcomes of the programme – how you do this is the subject of the next chapter.

Amount of learning

According to the NQF (QAA, 2001a, p. 6):

> The design of academic programmes has to make some assumptions about the amount of learning that is likely to be necessary to achieve the intended outcomes. In some cases this will be expressed in terms of study time, for example a number of academic years. In other cases this will be expressed through credit rating.

However (op. cit. p. 7):

> The qualifications framework itself does not specify minimum or typical volumes of learning by reference to units of credit … there is no single credit structure that is of universal application. The outcomes associated with a qualification should be understood in an holistic way, and their achievement should be demonstrated directly.

This is not particularly helpful to a module leader or even an institution. It is common in HE to use a tariff that:

> … provides a quantitative link between the number of credits which may be available within a notional learning time. 120 credits are normally attributed to the learning achievable in one full time academic year of approximately 30 weeks. 180 credits are normally attributed to one full time calendar year of approximately 45 weeks (InCCA, 1998, section 6.2.6).

> One credit is attributed to learning achievable in 10 hours of notional learning time (op.cit. section 5.4.2).

Your module will carry credit. How much and what that represents will be determined largely by your institution and the modular scheme it operates.

Thinking about your module

Are you aware of the benchmark statements for your subject area?

How does what you propose to teach fit with the knowledge section of the relevant benchmark statement?

Do you know the details of the programme specification(s) your module is part of, and how your module fits?

Levels of credit

Modular undergraduate schemes have in general used either two or three levels post A-level or post GNVQ (3). Some have also used a lower level equated with foundation studies, which are used to prepare suitable candidates for study at level 1. A number of schemes have been put forward which define descriptors for each level in a generally accepted way, but these are not 'yet' part of the NQF. The fullest sets were developed in Wales and by the Southern England Consortium for Credit Accumulation and Transfer (SEEC). SEEC's useful booklet *How to Use Learning Outcomes and Assessment Criteria* (Gosling & Moon, 2001) presents generic descriptors in the areas of:

- development of knowledge and understanding (subject specific);

- cognitive/intellectual skills (generic);

- key/transferable skills (generic); and

- practical skills (subject specific).

These are written at HE levels 1, 2, 3, masters and taught doctorate (NQF levels C, I, H, M and D). The first two, levels 1 and 2, are provided in Appendix 4, and show clearly levels of attainment and progression that may be expected of students through the HE system. If you are not familiar with writing specifications in learning outcomes form or with levels of credit, then Gosling & Moon (2001) is a good source book to use.

Volumes of credit

The volume of credit is more difficult to define than level since one credit corresponds to the outcome of 10 *notional* hours of study. The more common danger is to overload a module rather than make it lightweight but the concept of notional has to relate to the actual students expected on the programme. For example, students on a biology programme might take rather longer to complete a basic introduction to statistics than students on a statistics programme would. When basic modules are being used to service a number of different awards this issue should be addressed at the design stage.

Assessment in the national context

If outcomes are to be demonstrated then the assessment method must be such that students can actually demonstrate their understanding, their ability, and what they have been enabled to do. According to QAA (2001a, p. 7):

> Effective and appropriate assessment is essential to the operation of an outcomes-based qualifications framework. It is the assessment of the outcomes of learning that is important, rather than the nature of any component element of study.

The subject benchmarking statements help to relate the NQF to what happens in a module:

> At the programme or module level, benchmarking activities can focus on the types of programmes, the educational and training goals, intended outcomes and curricula content and these can be linked to the assessment process in terms of comparing strategies, assessment instruments, performance criteria and regulations (Jackson, 1998a, p. 8).

In Appendix 5 are extracts from two of the subject benchmark statements, allowing a comparison of specification of standards to be made that illustrates the different approaches in psychology (QAA, 2001b) and physics (QAA, 2001c). Although approaches to assessment and standards are listed, no attempt has been made to provide definitions of threshold (minimum) standards and modal (average) standards of achievement for students at module level

---

Thinking about your module

How much credit at what level will your module carry?

How many hours of study are you expecting from your students?

Will your students be on a single programme or on a range of programmes?

Can you identify any problems that might arise because of the diverse backgrounds of students starting the module?

---

although they are presented for award level. Despite all the detail, there is little on what instruments of assessment might be appropriate for establishing some of the detailed differences between threshold and modal performances which are specified, so professional academic judgement is still called for in interpreting what is specified. For example, how many problems do you need to complete to show 'an ability to solve problems in physics using appropriate mathematical tools'? How extensive does a student's knowledge have to be to qualify as 'knowledgeable about a number of specialised areas' in psychology?

In the framework documents however, there is a statement about the connection between the assessment of expected outcomes and the level of award which has implications for the assessment and the level of modules:

> For example, a student may, in an appropriate learning environment, build upon introductory material and be assessed against the outcomes of a qualification at a level above that associated with the introductory material alone (QAA, 2001a, p. 7).

The Code of Practice for the Assessment of Students

The Code of Practice for the Assessment of Students (QAA, 2000) has a series of clear, if broad, statements about what is acceptable practice for assessment:

> The principles, procedures and processes of all assessment should be explicit, valid, and reliable... Forms of assessment vary widely; however, in designing and operating its assessment processes, institutions will wish to consider:
>
> - how to make information and guidance on assessment clear, accurate and consistent and accessible to all staff, students, assessors and external examiners;

- the range and types of assessments used and how these measure appropriately the achievement by students of those skills, areas of knowledge and attributes identified as intended learning outcomes for the module or programme, and allow the strengths and weaknesses of the students to be demonstrated;

- how to ensure that assessment is operated fairly within programmes, and that the principles for assessment are applied consistently across the institution;

- how the reliability of assessment is demonstrated (for example, the consistent use of agreed marking and grading schemes, and moderation arrangements); and

- the robustness of arrangements to monitor, evaluate and demonstrate the fairness of assessments.

Institutional responsibilities

The Code of Practice further states a number of responsibilities that institutions should have with respect to assessment (p. 9). Some of these are obviously good practice implemented at institution level:

- ensuring that assessment is conducted with rigour and fairness, and with due regard for security; and

- publishing clear rules and regulations governing the conduct of assessment including deadlines for submission of assessed work.

Others will probably be devolved down to departments or subject groups for implementation:

- publishing, and implementing consistently, clear criteria for the marking and grading of assessments; and

- ensuring that there are robust mechanisms for marking and for the moderation of marks.

Others will become the responsibility of the module designer. These include ensuring that:

- the amount of assessment is consistent with an effective and appropriate measurement of the achievement by students of the intended learning outcomes and that it effectively supports learning; and

- due economy is exercised in the number of assessment tasks.

Finally, there are some that depend rather more on the structure of the modular scheme itself, which the individual module leader may be able to do little to control. These responsibilities include ensuring that:

- possible advantage of combining the assessment of a number of cognate modules is considered, to avoid assessment overload; and

- students have adequate time to reflect on learning before being assessed.

Thinking about your module

Are your familiar with the threshold and modal standards for your subject?

Do you know your institution's rules about assessment?

How will you go about designing assessment tasks that measure your students' achievement of the learning outcomes?

Do you (and your colleagues) have clear criteria for marking and grading?

Academic review

Most schools and departments in most HE institutions in the UK have been subject to academic review over the last six years. This QAA process 'looks at whether the aims and intended learning outcomes set for a programme are still valid'. Aspects of academic review that affect module designers include (QAA, 2001e):

- **reporting on academic standards**, which is concerned with the appropriateness of the intended learning outcomes (in relation to relevant subject benchmark statements, the qualifications framework and the overall aims of the provision); effectiveness of curriculum design and assessment arrangements (in relation to the intended learning outcomes); and the actual achievement of students; and

- **reporting on the quality of learning opportunities** which is concerned with the effectiveness of teaching, learning resources and academic support in promoting student learning and achievement.

As mentioned earlier in this chapter, the volume of learning will be a matter of concern (QAA, 2001a, p. 6, 7):

Providers of higher education programmes need to be able to demonstrate how the design of curricula secures academic and intellectual progression ... whether by a credit structure or otherwise. In this context, institutions should be able to demonstrate that the volume and nature of learning is adequate to achieve the outcomes indicated by the framework. Claims that those outcomes can be achieved from volumes of learning that are significantly below those found necessary by institutions generally, are likely to be tested by reviewers with particular thoroughness.

Assessment of students and their achievement will also be reviewed (QAA, 2001e):

- whether assessment is effective in measuring achievement of the outcomes; and

- whether student achievement matches the intended outcomes and the level of the qualification.

It is not clear at the time of writing how academic review will be organised beyond the immediate future. It seems reasonably clear, however, that module leaders will be held accountable for ensuring that benchmarks are used and interpreted appropriately when specifying programmes and designing and delivering modules.

Summary points

A module leader who is designing or rewriting a module description must be aware of the national context and must:

- understand the concept of level as used for both the NQF and the institution's credit framework;

- ensure that the outcomes specified in the module are consistent with those in the programme specification;

- use published academic standards in the subject area;

- use published benchmarks for assessment;

- use norms for the amount of learning that are shared by peers in other institutions; and

- recognise the importance, for Academic Review, of participating in the regular monitoring of the programme.

Designing a module – the institutional and school contexts

3

If you are designing a module it is not enough to know your subject, know how to teach and help others learn, know how to assess and be effective in routine administration. You must also understand how the modular system at your institution works, and the programme(s) in which your module sits. Chapter 2 reviewed the national context. This chapter considers common features of modular systems and the tensions they can create for module designers and for students. The first part of this chapter explores these features at the institutional level. The second part of the chapter looks at programme specifications, a school- or department- level consideration. If you are already familiar with these systems, you may want to go straight to Chapter 4, which is about designing modules that fit in award programmes.

Designing modules is dependent on teamwork

So you have to design 'your' module. Forget the idea that you will take your favourite topics and forge them into a series of beautifully coherent learning sessions over which you will rule and to which students – seeking knowledge and wisdom – will flock in sufficient numbers to allow the module to thrive. Your module doesn't exist in grand isolation – students will study it as part of a subject programme.

Working as part of a team can be a challenge if you are used to teaching in a non-modular system. You may feel that 'academic freedom' means that no one has the right to challenge what you do. You may be coming into university teaching after completing a research degree or with extensive professional experience, and you may be an experienced team player. But mastering the subject is not enough and having to fit within a whole new system can also be challenge.

Pitfalls await those who design their modules outside the team. One of the most miserable might be not attracting students, as this lecturer, new to a modular scheme, found:

> *I didn't realise that so few students would do my computer techniques option modules because most of the rest of their modules were compulsory.*

On the other hand, you need to be prepared if hundreds take your module, which happens on some business, statistics, and computing modules. You'll need to draw on the experience of the programme team when you're faced with collecting 300 mini projects with the same deadline and transporting them to your staff room to distribute to colleagues for marking. How will you know who hasn't handed a project in? How do you ensure they are all marked by an agreed date and returned to the students with feedback before the end-of-module exam?

What a module leader needs to know

Do you know… ?

- how much time students have to study your module;

- what level it is;

- which programmes it is part of;

- where it fits in a sequence of modules (if any);

- what knowledge and what skills a student needs in order to make a reasonable attempt at it;

- what knowledge or specific skills a student must learn in your module to prepare for any future modules which are dependent on it;

- how to specify what the module is about in terms of expected learning outcomes;

- what teaching patterns and assessment methods are allowed in your scheme;

- what assessment calendar is followed in your system; and

- what benchmarks exist in your subject area.

In designing and delivering a module you may well start with your subject specialism uppermost in your mind but hopefully you will want your module to be a 'good' learning experience for your students. From what is specified above (and in Chapter 2) you will realise that you cannot do that in isolation from your colleagues and without understanding how the modular scheme in your institution works.

Some of the worst problems we have found for module designers are presented in the table below.

Table 3.1: Problems for module designers

Cause	Effect	Typical observable problem
Very tight control of weekly timetable arrangements	Module designers cannot control lecture/seminar split and small group session times	Allocating appropriate staff to lead small groups very difficult; preferred length of sessions may not be possible
Very rigid control of term or semester structure	Only particular types of teaching or assessment can be used in particular weeks	Prevents use of different approaches, e.g. short answer tests in early stages of module
Very weak control of module delivery system	Insufficient flexibility in system for students to study modules across the institution	Leaves students with cancelled classes or re-arranged classes that they can't get to
Poor computer management system	Inadequate student records and class lists	Students don't know results; registration numbers not recorded; number and names of students registered on module is inaccurate

In the following sections we will look at the effects of timetabling and administrative bodies such as assessment boards that module designers should be aware of.

Rules, regulations and systems

Many problems blamed on modularisation have nothing to do with modularity per se but are caused by the central imposition of constraining, unhelpful and unnecessary administrative and/or management arrangements that seem designed to inhibit your preferred teaching methods. Priority is given to administrative convenience or standardisation rather than to teaching and learning. Seemingly arbitrary rules and regulations that the novice module designer may not anticipate include:

- rules about the length, width, shape and size of modules that prevent coherence or flexibility and limit the ability of different subject areas to achieve their unique goals;

- insufficient length of modules for conceptually complex topics that require gestation periods;

- the imposition of standard patterns of teaching (e.g. one lecture and one seminar a week per module) to control resources or introduce a spurious sense of equality between modules;

The numbers went up enormously – well I suppose they were designed to – but we were not prepared for coping with those kinds of numbers. We've fallen back on exams with multiple choice questions because we couldn't cope with the marking but the standard has definitely dropped.

- inflexible room timetabling systems that produce inappropriate pressure on teaching methods in order to fit the number and nature of rooms allocated rather than the educational needs of the module;

- enrolment regulations and systems that produce large and unpredictable variations in student numbers on modules, late arrivals and departures, totally disrupting the early weeks of a module;

- exam regulations that prevent the sensible and timely assessment of appropriate goals (e.g. no exams allowed in semester 1) or inappropriate methods (e.g. no coursework assessment allowed in semester 2);

- assessment board systems that cannot turn round grades in time to guide student module choice or allow planning for student numbers on subsequent modules; and

- administrative systems that work adequately within faculties but not across faculties, almost completely preventing the flexibility modularity was intended to bring.

In modular schemes that work well, a balance can be struck between competing 'local' and 'central' requirements, with sharing of responsibilities. Some examples are given in the table below.

Table 3.2: Balancing local demands and central arrangements

'Local' demands	Central arrangements
Flexibility in class time scheduled for a module	Need for each module to fill an equivalent time slot so flexibility in module choice possible
Special 'local' arrangements allowed in otherwise fixed pattern	Students may not be local and must be informed (and consulted?) by 'local' rather than central staff
'Local' room allocation to allow proper use of specialist accommodation	Central room booking to allow most efficient use of classroom accommodation

There is more room for workable compromises in systems that attempt to balance local and central requirements. Even so, you may encounter local demands that seem curious. Sometimes the patterns chosen locally have either been handed down without thought over the years, or arranged for the convenience of a member of staff, rather than because they are core requirements for a particular teaching and learning strategy!

Thinking about your module

If you are new to the university, talk with staff – both teaching and administrative –- who have been around for a while and who 'know the ropes'. Sometimes it's well worth learning from someone else's experience. The notes above may give you some ideas of the sorts of questions you might ask, and traps you might avoid when designing your module.

Rigid versus flexible timetabling

The following specification for a calendar grid was used by one institution in the early days of its modular scheme. The intention was to create flexibility by offering alternatives.

Table 3.3: Example of a rigidly constructed calendar grid

The calendar grid requires all modules that are all one size:
to commence at the beginning of one of weeks 2, 6, 11, 17, 21, or 26,
and to conclude at the end of one of weeks 5, 10, 14, 20, 25, or 29.

indicates module duration

week	2	3	4	5	6	7	8	9	10	11	12	13	14	15	16	17	18	19	20	21	22	23	24	25	26	27	28	29

The structure in this complex timetable was not suitable for students or staff. Students found too much variation in load per week because some modules lasted a short time and some a long time. Staff found that although there appeared to be flexibility the actual timings were too rigid and created problems for the use of specialist rooms.

A much simpler and more flexible timetabling system might set module lengths at one or two terms or semesters, with a common time period allowed for classes. For example, if on average the class time per module is 3 hours per week, the central system might be expected to use a repeat pattern of 3 hours. There is, however, no need to insist that all subjects use the same shape: arts might use a pattern of a 1-hour lecture plus a 2-hour seminar; science might have a 3-hour lab session;

business might have a 1-hour lecture, followed by 1 hour for group work and 1 hour for a seminar. It is even possible to turn a 3-hour session into two separate 75-minute sessions with a half hour break!

Booking class rooms within the timetable structure

In order that the institution can make the most efficient use of the finite pool of rooms of various sizes, you may have to take time slots you (and your students) don't want when seeking rooms for your module. Monday mornings and Friday afternoons are unpopular with everyone. Generally a subject group would be expected to spread its modules over the full week. In a balanced system, this means that those who allocate rooms must advise subject groups about the times at which different sized rooms are available. It also means that module leaders should request suitable rooms for their needs and class size.

Modular scheme assessment boards

The assessment board is a key central operator within the institution. One reason why assessment boards may not be operated 'efficiently' is because no one has thought through the implications of modularisation. In a scheme with a two-tier assessment board arrangement, information has to be provided so that students can be seen to have met the requirements for the award they are to be given. If the regulations are clear it is only the exceptional cases that need to be discussed.

Such modus operandi requires complete and accurate records that can be trusted. If the assessment board finds some module marks are missing confidence in the system is undermined and the records of some apparently failing students may have to be discussed in case there is an omission. The requirement for the board to have complete and accurate records of student marks/grades is a reason for the central imposition of hard deadlines for their submission by module leaders.

Another reason why hard deadlines are required for the submission of student grades is the role grades play in student choices about their modules for subsequent enrolment periods, as discussed in the next section.

Student choice and starting your module on time

I transferred during week two and then there was a timetable clash – I don't know why, as there wasn't supposed to be one – I missed the first four weeks and I just don't see how I can catch up.

Over-emphasis on student choice can be a cause of inefficiency in a modular system. Students may be permitted to change modules after the module leader has already received their list of enrolled students. This requires the module leader to make adjustments to the allocation of students to small groups, and perhaps even to repeat minor assessment tasks. A system that offers a high degree of module choice within an award must feed back to students their results for one term/semester before the deadline for choice for the next. If this is not done some students are bound to believe, after they see their results, that they would be better advised to register for a different module(s) and will want to change after the deadline. The advantages of late enrolment for students seems outweighed by the disruption it creates for both staff and other students.

Thinking about your module

Are you aware of the assessment board rules that will apply to your module?

Do you know what steps you need to take to ensure that you have suitable rooms for your classes?

Do you know how the time at which your module runs will be decided?

Living with modularisation

Modularisation tends to bring into the open issues that were not problems when courses were the units for resource allocation, and course managers made most of the decisions. If you do not see any advantages to yourself, your subject or your students in offering your programme as a set of modules, then these issues will continue to grate. Nevertheless, you owe it to your students to work to understand the system and deliver your subjects well within it. If you see some advantages for students in choice or for your programme structure in being able to offer alternative options or awards, then you have to recognise that there has to be a trade off between institution-wide overall patterns and local flexibility.

Subjects and award programmes

By the time you are writing a detailed module description, the programme specification should be available in draft. You may, of course, need to be involved in the preparation of the programme specification. QAA Guidelines (2001) provides some specific guidance, from which an extract is shown below (see also p. 10).

These guidance statements, whilst specifying as the norm much of what has traditionally taken place in HE courses, go further. The programme specification needs to show:

- an overall consistency with institutional policies such as those for the development of general skills;

- an awareness of subject standards in a national context by reference to benchmarks; and

- an overall coherence so that, for example, intellectual skills may be seen to be practised and demonstrated over a sequence of modules.

It also needs to be clear that individual assessments at the module level demonstrate the intended outcomes of the programme. An older generation may be reminded of the requirement of the Council for National Academic Awards (CNAA) to show 'coherence and progression' in modular schemes.

The QAA Guidelines seem to place the emphasis on specifying this coherence clearly rather than on the use of a specific method to do so. If

---

Some questions and answers about writing programme specifications – extract from QAA Guidelines (2001)

2   What reference points can we use to show that what we want students to achieve has currency within the academic, professional or employer communities?

- institutional mission statements and any institutional policies on the development of general skills in fields such as communication, information technology, team working and career management;

- subject benchmark statements;

- current research or other advanced scholarship carried out by academic staff;

- qualification descriptors used in the national qualifications frameworks...

3   How should we use subject benchmark statements?

... Benchmark statements are not intended to be draft specifications. Rather, they should be used as a point of comparison, a stimulus to reflection, and a reference against which individual programme specifications may be justified.

4   How do we expect our students to achieve and demonstrate the intended outcomes?

... Knowledge and understanding of a subject is often developed through lectures and seminars. Such direct teaching methods are usually supported by directed study of textbooks and journal articles (hard copy or electronic) and by assignment or project work. Knowledge and understanding is often assessed through unseen written examinations, but most if not all assessment methods will require some demonstration of knowledge and understanding.

Intellectual skills such as analysis, synthesis, evaluation, and problem solving may be practiced and demonstrated through more active learning processes involving assignments or projects, group-learning activity such as a seminar or tutorial, laboratory, workshop, or field-based activity. Assessment of intellectual skills can utilise unseen written examinations or problem-based exercises. Independent project work or research dissertations are typically used to demonstrate capability in a range of intellectual skills linked to specialist knowledge, understanding and practical skills.

Source: QAA Guidelines (2001), p. 6.

Fig. 3.1: An example of iterative planning

it is the case that coherence is of major importance, then an iterative process for planning a set of modules to create a programme, is particularly appropriate (see Figure 3.1).

Relationships between modules

It can be very helpful at the planning stage to show the relationships between modules and their prerequisites in the form of a simple diagram indicating the semester/term and year in which each module runs. This can be particularly useful when a module is part of several programmes (not least a single honours or major and a joint or minor), and as a reminder of the way in which skills and knowledge are expected to develop through the programme. Students can find such a diagram useful in their own programme planning when they have options with different prerequisites. To be of value, the diagram must be updated each time a module's prerequisites or delivery times are changed.

Programme specifications and student skills

There is considerable emphasis on the development of skills (both subject specific and general/transferable) in the QAA Guidelines for programme specifications. It is not too difficult to plan modules so that there is a coherent development of knowledge and understanding and of subject specific skills. It is more difficult, particularly in specifying one part of a joint degree or of a major-minor degree, or indeed in

I chose this module to fit in with my main subject – but it doesn't. They make no effort to relate it at all. I might as well have chosen nuclear physics.

specifying any award programme with option modules, to specify in module descriptions how the general/transferable skills will be developed. The QAA notes that 'Skills may be developed also through extra-curricular activities including work experience, student representative work, and social and cultural activities' (QAA Guidelines, 2001, p. 7). While skills development has to be specified at programme level, there are ways in which the development of these skills may be reinforced in the individual modules.

Using a skills matrix

One approach to incorporate skills into programmes is the skills matrix, which was introduced at Oxford Brookes University as part of the requirements for validation of an award. For each skill the modules in which it was taught or used or assessed were specified (see Figure 3.2). The matrix informs the module leader as to their responsibility for assessing or teaching a particular skill, and whether they could expect students to have particular skills already. For example, you may wish to use seminar presentations for both learning and assessment in your module that may be available to students in various schools or departments. You need to know if this is the first time students who take your module have been expected to give presentations. If they have to learn this skill it will affect your module planning. You also need to inform other module leaders that students will learn this skill in your module, and be assessed on it, and will come with this skill to future modules. The skills matrix enables you to make the skills associated with your module clear. Before the skills matrix was adopted at Brookes, module leaders often assumed that students would already have 'learnt' how to make a presentation and for some students, particularly those whose 'home subject' was elsewhere, this was not always the case.

Using skills modules

An alternative approach is to use specific modules for the development of both subject specific and general/transferable skills. At Gloucester University, students in their first full-time year must pass two skills modules as part of their studies. Briefly summarised, the purpose of the skills programme is twofold: to provide students with essential study skills, such as basic research methods, oral presentation and ICT skills; and to enable them to develop more advanced study skills specifically relevant to their fields or generally relevant to employment or later life (e.g. modern languages, problem solving, teamwork etc.). One module had a field/department focus, and was delivered by academic advisors. For the second module students could choose two six-week options designed to develop transferable skills in particular chosen areas.

Fig. 3.2: A skills matrix – localised discipline specific skills in psychology

Key: I = Introduced   P = Practised   (A) = Assessed

Module number	Analysing data	Applying psychological research	Clinical diagnosis	Dealing with cultural bias	Dealing with human subjects	Designing empirical studies	Ethics in psychology	Experimentation	Formulating research hypothesis	Introspection and account generation	Interviewing	Inferring motivations from behaviour	Observation	Personnel selection	Questionnaire and survey methods	(Computer) Simulation and modelling	Using statistical packages	Psychological testing	Writing psychological reports
1003	IP				IP	IP		I					IP		I				IPA
7701	I				IP	IPA		IPA		IP			IP						
7702	IP				IP	IPA	IP	I			IP		IP		I			IP	
7703	IP				IP	I		IP	IP				IP		I		IP		IPA
7710	P				P	P	IP	IPA	IP	IPA	IPA		IPA		IPA	IPA	P		PA
7712	IPA				IP	IP	IP	IP			IP		IP		IP			IP	IPA
7713		PA		IP			PA		P										
7715					IP		IP						P						PA
7721	PA		P			P	PA				P	IP			P				PA
7723	PA					P	PA	IA	PA	P			PA				P		PA
7725	PA					P		P	P						P			IP	PA
7726	PA					P	PA		PA	IP							P		PA
7730		P					I												PA
7735	PA					P	PA					P	P	I	PA		P	PA	PA
7736						P	PA	PA	IP				PA			IPA			PA
7737	PA	IP				PA	P			P	P		P		P		P		PA
7738	PA				PA	PA	PA						PA	I			P		PA
7739	IPA	PA				P	PA	PA	PA		P				PA		P		PA
779x	PA						PA		P								P		PA
8424	IPA				IP	IPA		IPA	IPA				I				IPA		IPA

> ## Thinking about your module
>
> What approaches to skills development are used in your school/department?
>
> Are you expected to develop and/or assess particular skills in your module?
>
> What skills can you expect students taking your module to have?

Problems arising from poorly planned programme specifications

The problems that arise from poorly planned programme specifications (which were discussed more broadly in Chapter 2) most often occur when the members of the staff team concerned inadequately understand the structure of the modular scheme. (It may also happen when staff are trying to resist modularisation.) Problems that module designers need to watch out for are:

- lack of coherence between sequences of modules students take, making it difficult to judge the level at which to start a module and to what extent the module should relate to other modules;

- lack of progression, and confusion about 'levels', especially within years 2 and 3, making it difficult to know whether the level the module is pitched at is appropriate;

- lack of coordination of students' learning experiences (e.g. too much group work all at once);

- differences in levels of intellectual demand between modules; and

- differences in workload between modules.

These problems most often happen if the members of the team do not understand the levels criteria in the credit framework or are failing to address the issues of overall planning and are concentrating entirely on individual modules. Familiarity with the credit framework discussed in Chapter 2 can be helpful in this situation.

Variations in subject demands and grading

Beyond the control of the subject programme designers, there may also be variations between different subjects to consider. These may not be catered for within the institution's codes of practice or protocols, but they may affect students who take your module but concentrate their studies in a different subject area. For example, there may be:

- differences in subject demands with which students have to cope, e.g. in writing conventions, and study pattern expectations; and

- differences in average marks and grade distributions between modules and subject areas – e.g. marks above 70% are commonly regarded as first class, but different subjects have different approaches to awarding marks over 75%. This can lead to major differences in honours classification when module marks from different subjects are averaged or aggregated.

Student evaluation and feedback may concentrate on the module and subject, so this effect on the overall student experience may go unnoticed. However, for the module designer, it may mean that for some students' time and attention has to be paid to the development of subject specific skills. It may mean that a different approach is needed to some aspects of assessment. It is better to take this on board at the design stage than wait until the module is being delivered to find out whether it is a problem.

Thinking about your module

Do you know how your module should relate to others in the programme(s)?

Do you know how the intellectual demands in your module compare to others in your subject area and to those in other subject areas your students might be studying?

Does your school/department have guidelines for defining the workload in modules?

Variations among students

Most students want to exercise choice to get the best results, to cover the most interesting or (to them) most important parts of the subject, and to prepare themselves for later employment or further study. Students may not end up in your module by choice. They may be there because:

- module choice may be more theoretical than actual and constraints of the system may mean the students have very little choice;

- poor guidance may have led a student to take your module mistakenly;

- grades and feedback from previous modules may have come too late to allow the student informed choice;

- the student's friend(s) might be doing the subject and they want to stick together; or

- your module is the most suitable given the timetabling choices available.

When designing your module, you need to consider how your module provides for students who are not properly prepared. Preparation includes not only suitable background knowledge but 'extras' such as study skills. As discussed above, these may be offered alongside courses, so that students develop them anyway. In other schemes there are no such courses because all resources follow student enrolment on modules and the 'extras' must be 'built in' to modules. Even students who enrol in your module because they find it the most exciting option available throughout the university may not bring the knowledge and skills to the module that you anticipate. Much of the rest of this book is devoted to helping you teach a diverse group of students in your classroom.

Other challenges

However good the modular system you have, a module leader is probably going to have to handle the following challenges:

- getting students 'up to speed' fast enough on short modules;

- tuning students in to the unique form of scholarship involved in one's discipline if this is their first (and perhaps only) experience of it;

- briefing students adequately and fast enough about what is involved;

- arranging intensive learning experiences (fieldwork, work placement, studio work) within conventional module shapes and sizes;

- matching external examiners' expertise to individual modules and avoiding an overload in terms of what they can reasonably see and moderate;

- coping with large groups of students within introductory and popular open access modules;

- an increase in the volume of marking; and

- lack of clarity about where responsibility lies, leading to major issues being dropped and ignored and lecturers retreating to the teaching of their individual module.

The good news is that these challenges are not insurmountable and the following chapters give ideas for dealing with them. It does, however, make sense to expect them at the design stage and to try to build in to your module the flexibility or structures that you need to use the appropriate methods.

Summary points

As an effective module designer you should be able to:

- work with a team of colleagues to develop a programme specification and plan a set of modules;

- recognise the constraints on module structure and delivery imposed by the modular scheme within which you will operate;

- devise assessment tasks and timetables within the constraints imposed by the assessment boards;

- plan for the uncertainty in student numbers on your module and the effects of students joining the module after it has started;

- cope with varied and unpredictable background knowledge and skills of students on modules, especially in lectures; and

- integrate the development of students' skills, as specified for the programme, into you own module.

Designing your module

4

In this chapter the focus is on designing your module. It provides an overview of the considerations you need to keep in mind when working out how students will best learn your subject. It provides an overview of writing learning outcomes, choosing teaching methods and setting suitable assessments. Chapters 2 and 3 have looked at how national, institutional and school/department imperatives will affect how you think about and plan your module. This chapter is about what you need to do to put the module together.

How you design your module has much to do with your educational philosophy, which may be something you haven't thought about all that much. Designing a module that helps your students learn well is not necessarily easy. Further, new lecturers are often expected to take over existing modules and/or to teach to a curriculum defined by professional bodies.

An outcomes-based approach

This book, like the QAA, takes an outcomes-based approach: your module should be defined by learning outcomes the achievement of which can be assessed. To develop learning outcomes you need to get the curriculum in focus. Biggs (1999, pp. 33–53) says that to get this focus you need to do the following:

- decide what kind of knowledge is to be involved (knowing about something or how to do something based on knowledge);

- select the topics to teach, being careful not to try to 'cover' everything but to provide for depth of understanding of essential content;

- clarify the purpose of the module, and therefore what is most important for students to understand, to prioritise the topics you will cover; and finally

- put the objectives or learning outcomes together in relation to assessment tasks so that you can report the students' results of learning as a grade.

What module leaders need to be able to do

To design your module you need to have knowledge of the national, institutional and school contexts, and the following:

- the requirements for documentation, both for student guidance and learning and for validation and review;

- the different backgrounds of students and the consequential differences in their experience and knowledge;

- the assessment schedule and associated workload and their relation to those of other modules;

- the links between modules;

- the students' needs for feedback; and

- the significance of the module in different programmes.

This knowledge needs to inform the learning and teaching strategy that is adopted and means that a module leader needs to be able to:

- describe modules appropriately, identifying prerequisite skills and knowledge required, learning processes involved, learning outcomes expected and content covered, to brief students and to enable them to make an informed choice if their programme allows it;

- provide substantial documentation about how the module operates – in terms of learning processes and expectations for use of study time, assessment tasks and criteria etc., as well as timetables and contents;

- help students get up to speed fast with an induction into the topic and a way of engaging with it;

- help students develop the skills needed to tackle the learning tasks the module involves;

- identify and communicate the help that is available to students to develop the prerequisite skills or knowledge if they do not have them;

- schedule assessment and workload in ways that do not clash with other modules which are likely to be taken by the students during the same semester or term;

- provide quick and early feedback on student progress;

Isn't the use of learning outcomes a very reductionist process? The problem .. is that if learning is indefinable it becomes impossible to assess it!

Gosling & Moon (2001)

- pay explicit attention to links between modules;

- provide social glue to bind students into the module and create a sense of belonging;

- provide alternative tasks and assignments for students from different areas to link the module to their main areas or to personal interests; and

- adopt conventions (e.g. assessment tasks and criteria, formats of teaching sessions) which students find familiar because they are adopted across a programme or pathway.

In those courses in which students are allowed to register for a module after the learning and teaching programme is underway it is in addition important to:

- provide an early overview and sample of process to allow students to make decisions to drop out and transfer (or to stay with it); and

- provide easy ways for those who transfer in late to pick up speed.

On top of all this a module leader is often expected to:

- build in ways of identifying students, especially in large modules with little tutorial contact, in case special circumstances are made known or cases of plagiarism or cheating are identified or individuals need additional help; and

- have an awareness of what students are doing in the rest of their study time on other modules in terms of topics, tasks and assessment deadlines.

Your institution or faculty or department may of course have its own guidelines, practices and support systems for some of these matters which the module leader must know about, tap into and refer students to.

All in all this seems a daunting list. Do you still want to be a module leader?

If students made a real mess of the first and only assignment in week seven then it was too late to sort out the problems. Now we use an early assignment just to orient them a bit better. I think you have to get them confidently on track early on if you are going to make much progress in such a short course.

Essential components of your module design

Important steps in designing your module are:

- identify the aims of the module (what is the purpose of this module?);

- write learning outcomes;

- design assessment tasks that will test whether students have achieved the learning outcomes;

- develop or identify criteria for grading the assessment;

- decide on a teaching and learning strategy that will enable the students to achieve the learning outcomes; and

- work out a schedule of classes and assessment tasks.

All these aspects of your module should be organised in a module description and guide.

A proforma for a module description

Many institutions have module proformas that you are required to follow. An outline of a module proforma is shown in Figure 4.1. If your institution does not have one, it is well worth agreeing with your colleagues that you will develop one for your modules. You will find it helps you:

- avoid making assumptions that you discover too late are not shared;

- avoid omitting essential information; and

- present information consistently so it is easy to follow.

Fig. 4.1: A proforma for a module description

1	Factual information	Title, number, size, shape, level, semester / term in which it runs
		Award programme(s) or paths, pre- and / or co-requisites
		Intended learning outcomes
		Summary description and context, including description of teaching and learning strategies
2	Content and coverage	Knowledge and understanding
		Subject specific skills and methodologies
		Transferable skills (taught, used and / or assessed)
3	Assessment regime	Exam and / or coursework weighting
		Special requirements or conditions (e.g. must pass both components of assessment)
4	Date of approval (validation)	

Writing learning outcomes

Gosling and Moon (2001) provide a concise argument in favour of using learning outcomes and assessment criteria:

> By linking learning outcomes with assessment criteria and assessment practice, greater coherence in curriculum design can be achieved. Teaching strategies need to be developed which will enable the student to achieve the learning outcomes and meet the requirements of the assessment criteria. When they are written in relation to level descriptors as well, they provide a coherent picture of where a module fits in the hierarchy of modules that make up a programme.
>
> Well written learning outcomes provide a means of mapping the content of a curriculum – for example, to see how they reflect benchmark statements, which of the key skills are acquired, where the same skill or content is appearing more than once in the programme, the capabilities the students acquire as they progress through the levels in the programme of study (Gosling & Moon, 2001, p. 11).

Figure 4.2 shows Gosling and Moon's (2001) model for module/ programme development.

It is important to understand that learning outcomes have to be something that the student can 'do', so that they can be assessed. Stating that a student should know or understand x or y is not something that you can assess. You can only assess a demonstration of that knowledge, which may be through comparing ideas in an essay, using a range of communication skills to share a plan, or designing a model village with efficient transport systems. Learning outcomes require verbs to describe the behaviour that demonstrates a student's learning, and information about the context for that demonstration.

A commonly used framework for defining levels of learning is Bloom's taxonomy which has six levels of cognitive learning outcomes: knowledge, comprehension, application, analysis, synthesis and evaluation. When writing learning outcomes for HE the higher levels of learning – application, synthesis and evaluation of knowledge – must be included.

Jude Carroll, Staff and Education Developer at Oxford Brookes University, makes the following points about learning outcomes to participants in the Certificate in Teaching in Higher Education, at Brookes:

> *Learning outcomes define what the student is expected to learn as a result of taking your course, and what they will do to show you and other authorities that they have learned it. They also define standard or quality of learning. Learning outcomes have three parts:*

Fig. 4.2: Model for module/programme development

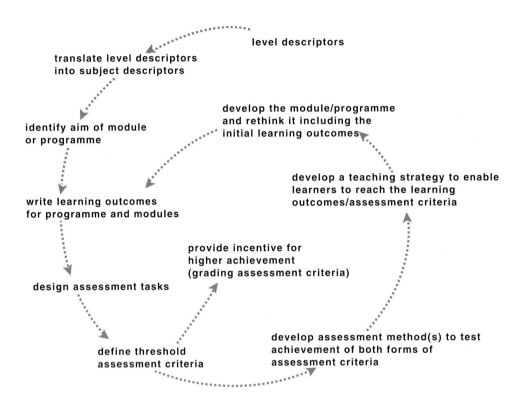

Source: Gosling & Moon (2001) How to Use Learning Outcomes and Assessment Criteria. *London: SEEC, p. 15.*

- *what the student will do that demonstrates learning;*

- *in which context the student will demonstrate learning; and*

- *how well the student will demonstrate this learning.*

Following this approach, here is one example of a learning outcome with each of the three parts highlighted:

The student will be able to draft, with guidance from others, a funding application likely to be successful in seeking funds from a variety of sources.

1 what the student will do – draft an application

2 in which context – with guidance and using a variety of sources

3 how well s/he will do it – likely to be successful.

Module summary

In a marketing degree programme the module on international behaviour was described as:

An examination and explanation of the issues raised by marketing in an international context.

In contrast the module on buyer behaviour was described as:

An introduction to and exploration of the main theories and concepts underlying our understanding of buying decision making processes (consumer, industrial and institutional) applied primarily in a business and marketing context. The conceptual foundations of the course derive from its basis in the social sciences. Concepts and applications are linked throughout the course and assignments are designed to aid students in applying behavioural principles to marketing problems.

Module summary

It is worth making your summary as explicit as possible – it may well prove to be the main information on which student choice is based. Don't just include a few headings from the content or a few words that are in addition to the module title, but show how your module relates to the programme specification. Chapter 3 considers this in more depth.

Assessment regime

A common problem for a module leader is to simply specify the assessment as exams or coursework, or a bit of both, adopting methods commonly used in the subject area. A better approach is to begin by determining learning outcomes. It then becomes much easier to design assessment tasks appropriate for demonstrating that students have achieved particular outcomes. There is also a need to separate the assessment from the learning it is intended to promote and define and to think in terms of assignments that can be used to demonstrate a number of outcomes. Clear and helpful criteria describing how the assessment task will be graded should also be devised, generally through collaboration of the whole course team, and made available to students.

In brief, what is required of the assessment system is:

- a carefully planned number of occasions where marks are allocated;

- an agreed measure of the amount of work a student should need to spend on assessment in an average module;

- assignments that capture appropriate amounts of student effort;

- assignments that generate appropriate forms of learning activity;

Our documentation is so much better than it used to be. You realise how much of what went on in the past was implicit and you have to make it explicit. It's enormously reduced the number of students knocking on my door and I think we've thought things through better, too.

- assignments that can be assessed readily and unambiguously within the time available to staff; and

- regular, timely and influential feedback on student learning.

Thinking about your module

Providing good documentation is worthwhile for a number of reasons. A concise module summary may mean that students arriving in your module know what to expect. Clearly written learning outcomes linked to appropriate assessment tasks also convey much about a module to prospective students. Imagine that you are an interested student reading your module summary. Consider asking current students if the module summary reflects their experience of your module.

The amount of assessed work required from a student who is to complete successfully their programme must take into account classification, transcripts and 'what graduates should be able to do'.

Assuming each module will be assessed, the minimum 'size' of a module is important: too many small modules will increase the number of distinct pieces of work that have to be assessed even if the amount of time taken is effectively controlled. Within a module consideration must be given both to the number of separate assignments and to their size.

The amount of student effort required to complete assignments for assessment should be planned as part of module design in the context of the total number of learning hours allocated to the module and not left to chance.

It is also worth re-quoting a QAA statement (2001e) about assessment that is presented under the heading 'Academic review' in Chapter 2:

Assessment of students and their achievement will also be reviewed:

- whether assessment is effective in measuring achievement of the outcomes; and
- whether student achievement matches the intended outcomes and the level of the qualification.

There is more on assessment in Chapter 7.

> ## Checklist
>
> Below is a summary checklist of some of the issues that need to be addressed when designing and delivering modules:
>
> - lack of coherence between sequences of modules students take;
>
> - lack of progression, and confusion about 'levels';
>
> - coping with larger groups of students;
>
> - coping with varied background knowledge and skills of students;
>
> - tuning students in to the form of scholarship involved in one's discipline;
>
> - rushed assessment, bunched assignment deadlines and late feedback to students;
>
> - increase in the volume of marking; and
>
> - difficulty of building in 'extras' such as study skills.

Some useful tips

Four ways in which teaching and learning on modules (other than those that last for more than a semester) is different from teaching and learning on linear courses are:

- the speed with which students need to get to grips with the subject matter;

- the diversity of student background and experience;

- assessment and feedback; and

- evaluation.

These issues are dealt with in Part 2. They will be found to contain ideas that can be incorporated into modules at the design stage as well as approaches that can be adopted as teaching strategies whether or not they are specified in a module description. However, if your scheme allows it you will find you retain more flexibility in your approach if you:

- avoid overemphasising the use of lectures for teaching knowledge and understanding – you may find you want to divide students into groups depending on their backgrounds and use a workbook to develop at least some of the knowledge and understanding;

- avoid specifying what the small group activities will be but give exemplars – for example you may find you want to try out some new ideas which involve teamwork when that wasn't part of your original plan;

- give exemplars of assignments or assessment methods rather than a fixed statement – you may find you want to try something new to you such as peer assessment; and

- ensure that the book or resource list is illustrative – you may find you want students to access world wide web sources that were not on your initial list.

Summary points

As a module leader or designer, it is important that you:

- identify the aims of your module in relation to the programme(s) it is part of;

- identify what documentation is required;

- present the expected learning as outcomes;

- design appropriate learning and assessment opportunities and tasks; and

- devise teaching and assessment schedules that fit the programme and institutional contexts.

Getting going

5

Part 2 is all about delivering your module. This chapter concentrates on getting going; Chapter 6 explores ways to cope with – even thrive on – student diversity; Chapter 7 has advice and tips for managing marking and feedback; and Chapter 8 is about ways to use your module evaluation effectively.

Starting a module

Both students and module leaders face challenges when starting a module. The student has to get to grips with the methodology, content and culture of the subject, get to know the staff and other students. One student commented:

> Everyone new to the subject was linked up with someone who was studying it as their main subject. I was paired off with Gina and she's been brilliant. I don't know how I'd have survived without her.

The module leader has to know which and how many students are on the module and to ensure that they are all briefed appropriately about the module. One member of staff commented:

> The unpredictability of student numbers is a killer. Almost the only thing you can guarantee about the first few weeks is that there will be chaos.

Session one day one is the time to get to grips with these problems else delay may begin to demotivate the good students who expected to start straightaway. They can be tackled by three linked strategies:

- briefing students about the module;

- inducting students into the module; and

- creating social cohesion.

You need to have planned how you will create small groups, and begin with activities to get students involved fast. This chapter focuses on these issues, with some specific examples of useful teaching strategies.

Briefing students about the module

Most institutions have a guide to modules offered. It may be at institutional, or faculty or subject/departmental level. In most cases, the guide will comprise the summaries that form part of the validated module description so these should be as explicit as possible. If a student doesn't have much prior knowledge of the subject matter or doesn't know the approach to expect, an explicit, informative description should make it easier for the student to decide whether or not to take the module. One of the most disrupting and difficult-to-manage features of any module is to have a substantial number of students joining late because they have had to de-register from a different but 'wrong' module. It is worth trying to ensure that your own module description doesn't lead to late enrolment on other modules.

For students who are making choices within a restricted range of modules in a single subject area, the information may need to be far fuller and may be provided by making module guides available. These guides may also have details about assessment patterns and types of assignment. This information will help those students who make a choice based on assessment type or style rather than on content. Some students may wish to develop a particular personal skill and choose a module that will enable them to do this. As far as possible it is preferable to provide all this information and encourage students to use it when choosing modules as this should reduce the number who register and then de-register because it is not the 'right' module.

In general a **module guide** should be similar to a **module description** (see Chapter 4) with additional and more practical information about the particular delivery of the module (e.g. actual dates of events or deadlines rather than week numbers). How much of this information is available to students before they start the module depends on local practice and the type of modular programme that is offered.

Programme guides

Some information about the methodology or approach to be used may apply to a group of modules or even a complete programme rather than a single module. In these cases it is worth collecting material to create a subject guide. This approach seems to be expected in the QAA Guidelines (2001) although the only example (see opposite) does not have **detailed** information about individual modules. The information in the extract does, however, show what information a student who is only doing one of the human geography modules might need.

Unless module leaders deliberately step outside their own subject, they may not realise how different is the approach to, say, writing a practical

What a degree in human geography means at Gloucester University – teaching, learning and assessment methods

The curriculum is designed to enable you to acquire and develop your subject knowledge and understanding, thinking, practical and key life skills... As you progress through the Levels you will be encouraged to expand your understanding and critical appreciation of key human geographic topics. For example, in the analysis of economic geography issues the scale of analysis shifts from the global to the national to the local as you progress... In all your studies in human geography you will apply theory to case study analysis.

.... You will attend lectures, participate in seminars and tutorials and carry out practical work, both in class time and out in the field. You will work independently through guided study and use the Internet and computer assisted learning packages. Practical work and fieldwork will give you the opportunity to work in groups while at the same time prepare you for independent fieldwork. ... You will also participate in group work aimed at developing your ability to work co-operatively with others. You will receive worksheets created to help and direct you in the use of your private study time. Through independent study you should increase your understanding of issues covered in formal class time.

A variety of assessment methods are used in human geography. Most modules will have two pieces of assessment which may include essays, reports (individual or collective), posters, 'sample' articles, diaries, field notebooks, literature reviews and seminar papers, seen and unseen examinations. Assessment methods give you the opportunity to demonstrate your understanding of issues to the highest level and your ability to use specialist study skills. Several modules which are of a practical nature do not have an examination; assessment in these modules is usually via staged coursework and can include computer tests, field notebook, oral presentations and Internet work. Some group work related to fieldwork may be assessed via an oral presentation, this work is normally marked by staff and other students in your class, and through the submission of a group or individual report...

Source: QAA Guidelines (2001, p. 28) example 4C programme specification written for students

report in physics from writing one in psychology, or in ecology from chemistry. Students on joint honours courses can sometimes have unnecessary problems if these differences are not spelt out at the outset of a module.

Assignment guides

It may also be useful to have an assignment guide. This spells out what is required in each assignment and clarifies the criteria by which the assignment will be assessed and the weighting of different components of the assignment (e.g. the bibliography or quality of presentation). If students from different academic backgrounds are taking the same module it may also be helpful to give examples of what is meant by different terms used since different subjects have significantly different assessment cultures.

Module guides on the web

It is worth looking at the possibility of setting these guides up as web pages. Word-processed guides can easily be formatted as web pages and made available on the programme web site. This technique makes it much easier to ensure that everyone has the current guide. You will need to give some thought to layout since pages formatted for printing are not necessarily easy to follow when presented online. Students may not want to print their own copies because of the cost. They may, however, be quite prepared to download them into their own PCs, so you may need to make sure that there is a file transfer facility. If you have a large number of students, publishing module guides on the web may enable you to avoid the very considerable logistic problem of distributing several hundred copies of the document in a lecture theatre which may be on a different site from your office!

Providing good quality information to students before they register can help to decrease the number of students who want to change their registrations in the first week that the module runs. Achieving such a decrease must be worthwhile for students and staff.

Inducting students into the module

If you have students from other study backgrounds on your module they will need help to understand the approach used in the module and subject area. They may need to be briefed in detail about the conventions that are used. It may be possible to group students from other subject areas with a student from the module subject area. This 'subject specialist' can then be a first point of reference for students encountering something unfamiliar. If they are willing, such guiders can be explicitly identified.

In other cases it may be better to put students into groups that are expected to provide mutual help. This prevents particular individuals being exploited but will only work if the group is given help by the module leader to establish working relationships. Groups that are left to 'get on with it' without guidance or set tasks are rarely effective unless they have worked together before or a particular member is sufficiently experienced to enable the group to provide the tasks and modus operandi for themselves.

It was really confusing at the beginning. Everything was different – the seminars, the way you are supposed to write. No one explained how it worked – they assumed you already knew.

46

Creating social cohesion

In conventional courses normal social mechanisms allow students to establish their own social groups within the limits of the course contacts and mode of study. In modular courses, students may not encounter the same students from one module to the next. More particularly, part-time students often find it difficult to socialise with other students outside the teaching sessions. Informal social groups can be a useful aid to support student learning but if the circumstances are not right for them to form naturally they may have to be engineered. The Open University, for example, has had summer schools in which the largely independent learners have been able to interact and socialise with others on the same course. In some distance learning courses an equivalent contact group is provided electronically for students who may never meet face to face.

Although your module may have lectures that all students attend and no physical barriers to social cohesion, it may still suffer from the fact that these groups take time to form, develop and cohere. It is then important for you to foster such social interaction by encouraging teamwork in different situations. For example, a team may tackle a particular project either as a paper exercise or as a real task. Seminars or problem classes may be based around participants working in teams rather than as individuals. Interaction in lectures may be encouraged as a learning exercise and facilitated through teams or small groups.

Using small groups

When creating seminar groups you need to bear in mind what the group will be required to do. You may have to choose between establishing groups of students with similar learning backgrounds and interests or with diverse backgrounds. It may be better to try to ensure that a group has students from a number of backgrounds so that different aspects of a topic may be presented by a student with an appropriate background.

I really enjoy the way students from other subjects ask difficult questions. It has livened up the seminars no end and I set more interesting essay questions.

Energy sources

This module was taken by students with backgrounds in physics and chemistry, and by students on single honours and joint honours degrees. Seminar groups were constructed so that each included both physics and chemistry students and a biology or social sciences student. This helped the physical sciences students to understand the broader social background and the other students to grasp some of the technical details involved in moving to wind power or other greener sources.

Group work and grading

One area in which particular care should be taken when expecting students to work in groups for an assignment, is how such work may be carried out within the institution's regulations covering cheating, plagiarism and syndication. It obviously needs to be made clear how this should be done so that co-operation and syndication can be readily distinguished. In some areas students, though working in a group, will be expected to produce their own piece of work for assessment. In others peer review is used to decide how the group mark should be allocated to each individual on the basis of the contribution that each has made. In this situation, the module leader should make some provision for an individual to present arguments or explanations as to why mark allocations might be invalid.

The module leader is responsible for ensuring that there is no discrimination on non-academic grounds in any aspect of the student experience in their module. If such problems are not dealt with, a student's only way forward in a matter of dispute may be through the formal complaint or academic appeal procedures. Peer and other non-traditional assessment techniques can be valid and reliable, but it is important to recognise that they can also lead to dispute.

Traditionally many staff in HE have enjoyed the dialogue and interaction they have had with 'their' students and some have come to associate the difficulty of continuing this practice with modularity. Reduction in one-to-one contact (if it has been reduced) is more likely to be a result of the reduction of resources for increased student numbers than the introduction of modularity per se. There is no reason why modules should not be based on small group teaching if sufficient resources are assigned. In fact most universities that operate modular schemes offer honours degrees with project, dissertation or independent study modules that are carefully structured to allow student learning to be supported by one-to-one contact or small group teaching.

Teaching strategies for getting going fast

There is no way you can get through the syllabus in the way we used to so I go for oomph. I start with a bang, focus the whole module around the central idea and then tie it up tight at the end.

As modules are generally only a term or semester long, students need to get going quickly, adopting appropriate patterns of study and orienting themselves to the central issues of the module. One of the best ways of getting students into your module quickly is to give them an immediate experience of the kinds of learning task they will be involved in. Often modules start with many weeks of lectures or background that fails to engage students – they may be turned off before they get to the project or other active tasks later on. The more quickly students get a taste of what your module will entail, the more quickly they can transfer to another module if yours is not what they are looking for.

To get going fast and help students become acclimatised to the academic culture of your subject, it is a good idea to start with an overview or sampler. Samplers can also be used as a vehicle for establishing relationships between students, especially where group activities are employed. If these activities are not assessed, they are more likely to encourage open co-operation. It is important to take a little time to debrief the students about their experiences of the samplers you offer. This can help them to recognise what they should spend their time on and how they can best go about the main learning tasks involved in the module.

Overview lecture

The first lecture can be used to summarise the content of the module:

- the list of lecture topics and their interrelationships;

- the key issues addressed in the course; and

- the kinds of problems (and assessment tasks or exam questions) students will be able to tackle by the end.

Such a lecture can provide a mental map of the territory to be covered in the module and make it easier for students to see where they are going and to relate components to each other. It is possible to use the first session to outline the content and process of the main learning activities students will be engaged in:

- the seminar topics or set essay questions;

- the laboratory sessions; and

- the project or other extended assignment.

In the example below, the first session – a four-hour slot – was used to engage students in the central issue of the module through a variety of processes including discussion, brainstorming, a lecture, a video, and the formation of project groups and selection of group tasks.

Trial assignment

If a module consists primarily of a series of assignments, possibly even weekly learning tasks (such as tackling problem sheets, analysing legal cases or reading for seminars), the first week can be used as a 'dry run' to induct students into the process of the module. Students can learn how to undertake the main learning activities in a way that will set them up for the whole module.

Contemporary Chinese politics – an overview

This module started with a four-hour session involving the following components:

- students read newspaper accounts of the Tiananmen Square protests and massacre of June 1989, engaged in a brainstorm session about what caused it, and from these ideas the class as a whole identified preliminary causative factors such as 'struggle for political succession' and 'impact of western ideas on students';

- building on this, the lecturer explained how the course is organised around the central question of why the Tiananmen Square events took place, that there would be an examination question on this issue and that each student would be in a project group to research one of the possible explanations;

- a 'Panorama' programme from July 1989 about Tiananmen Square was shown; and

- research topics were identified and project teams were established. By the end of the first session both the central content and the process of the module had been clearly established.

Mini-project

Often the main learning activity of the module or the final activity the module builds up to is a project of some kind – a field trip, an extended experiment or an extended piece of research and writing. While it is possible simply to brief students about such a project at the outset of the module, they may forget about it as they get stuck into the early lectures or practical work and find themselves ill-prepared and short of time when they encounter the project later in the module. It can be very effective to undertake a small-scale version of this project as the very first activity on the module – simulating every aspect of the activity on a smaller scale with a much shorter time scale. Such mini-projects provide

Psychology of learning – a sampler

In a module involving paired seminar presentations and peer assessment of the presentations, the first week was used to demonstrate the processes involved. The normal 'assignment' involved two students preparing for and running a one-hour long session for a group of 12. In the 'dry run' in the first week, six pairs of students each took responsibility for a 15-minute slot and prepared and gave a mini-seminar. Two hours were allocated for this initial session. The topics, reading, seminar and peer assessment were all scaled down but involved exactly the same elements as in subsequent weeks. In the first week a tutor attended each session and concentrated on students learning how to read appropriately, how to prepare seminars, how to present them and handle questions and discussion, and how to give and receive peer feedback. In subsequent weeks the tutor did not attend all the seminar sessions but dropped in on several of the parallel sessions to check that they were operating satisfactorily.

very effective and vivid briefing and also alert students to the planning and time involved. Mini-projects can also be very engaging and successful in capturing student attention at a time in the semester when most modules have hardly got going.

Content mapping project

It can be valuable for students to research and summarise the content of the module for themselves and to 'map' it so as to be able to develop a succinct overview. Such 'maps' can take the form of patterned notes (or organic notes or 'spider' diagrams), poster summaries, diagrams or conventional list-like notes. The first week of the module can be devoted to such a research and summarising activity, which is often best undertaken co-operatively in small groups. This activity can also assist social cohesion as well as exploit different knowledge backgrounds and interests of students. Lecturers can comment on students' overviews, present their own and highlight the areas and approaches the module will take, the significance of which might have been lost without the prior activity of mapping the content. In the example below many of the students had a very limited background knowledge and were asked to summarise the whole of Italian history on one side of a sheet of paper!

Introduction to Italian history

Previously students of Italian history had begun the course by listening to a lecture on 15th century Italy. With modularisation many of the 80+ students arrived with little or no background in Italian history, culture, politics or even basic geography. They lacked an overview within which specialised lectures could be located. The module was revised and then began with a week-long exercise in which groups were required to draw up a summary of the entire social, political and cultural history of Italy from 1400 to the present day on a single A1-sized poster, with a 'time line' running from left to right across the sheet. Students with different backgrounds were deliberately mixed and students within groups were encouraged to select topics for research with which they were not already familiar. They were briefed for the exercise in an introductory session, pointed to information sources in the library and elsewhere, and then spent a week independently researching and summarising. In a session in week two, all groups displayed their posters on the walls of a lecture theatre and 'toured' the posters looking at other groups' summaries. This was followed by an overview lecture and comments from the lecturer on the posters as a briefing for the more specialised lectures which would follow.

Day one exam

Stating the expected learning outcomes for a module sometimes fails to communicate what a module is really about or what kind of 'performance' students will be expected to give at the end. In contrast a 'mock' exam can give an alternative overview, an extremely vivid, if

51

alarming, impression of what the module really entails. The first seminar or problem class can be put aside for a mock exam – possibly involving a sample of questions or shorter questions than in the final exam. This focuses students' minds on the scale and nature of the task facing them very effectively. To get the most from such a device it can be helpful to:

- explain to students that they are not being assessed but being given an impression of what the module really entails, and that in the past most students have been able to tackle such questions perfectly adequately by the end of the module;

- encourage students to have a go at questions even if they initially feel they know nothing – it is often the case that they know more that is relevant than they realise and it is useful to recognise what they already know or can bring from other modules they have already taken; and

- encourage students to recognise the topics involved in the exam questions that are not covered in the module – the prerequisite knowledge students should already possess – and to make a note of the topics they need to catch up on quickly.

Summary points

As a module leader wanting to get going well, it is important that you ensure that potential students have good, clear information about your module, its methodology and assessment activities before registering. At week one you need to:

- understand the (diverse) academic backgrounds of your students;

- have a suitable opening session for the module prepared; and

- organise small groups effectively.

Coping with student diversity

6

This chapter explores the sorts of difficulties module leaders might encounter that arise from student diversity, and suggests solutions. On modular courses, students may come from a variety of study backgrounds with a wide range of knowledge, understanding and skills. You need to be able to integrate all these students and provide good learning experiences for them. On the positive side, your module may well be greatly enriched by the diversity of learning your students bring with them.

Many modules have knowledge prerequisites, whether specified in terms of prerequisite modules or of content students should be 'familiar with'. However in some modular systems these prerequisites are advisory only, defining the starting point for the module. In others the module leader is allowed to permit students without the prerequisites to register and is then duty bound at least to advise them about the gaps in their learning.

> We've had a lot of arguments about prerequisites. If we increase our prerequisites it is easier to teach modules because you can rely on similar levels of background knowledge but then we go broke because too few students can take our modules. I don't think we have resolved this yet.

Students then, may arrive on modules without the knowledge and skills they require to benefit fully, or even at all, from the module. If this happens, the student might be best advised to take an alternative module or to undertake some additional background work before commencing the module. This is clearest in mathematical and scientific areas with hierarchical knowledge structures but it can also be the case in the social sciences. Advice and direction to background work is most effective where there is clear evidence of a lack of crucial background knowledge and skill.

Pretests

One way of obtaining the necessary 'evidence' about a students' existing knowledge and skills is to arrange a brief pretest. It may be possible to provide a self-administered and scored test to students intending to enroll on a module so students who lack the prerequisites can refer themselves elsewhere. It may be necessary to administer such a pretest at the start of the module whilst a student still has time to withdraw from your module and register for a different module. Whenever such a test is administered it should lead to clear diagnosis, rather than just a score, and students should be unambiguously directed to targeted remedial material or have remedial tuition provided where appropriate.

Optional tutorials

The key strategy for coping with diverse needs is to target support where it is needed rather than to give everybody everything 'just in case'. It is much more efficient to offer a range of tutorial opportunities that only a minority of students make use of than to have tutorials for everybody that few gain from because they are so poorly focused. Where students have regular feedback on their progress (for example through regular testing) they are in a good position to refer themselves to optional tutorials addressing the specific topics they need help with.

In the introductory physics module example see page 59, students sat weekly multiple choice question tests and referred themselves to optional problem classes targeted on the questions answered incorrectly by the largest number of students. They could also sign up for 10-minute 'surgery' slots to discuss questions they still did not understand. Where students do not have good diagnostic information on their progress and have not identified specific problems they are much less likely to make use of such optional sessions. (See also the example for introductory chemistry in Chapter 7, p. 81.)

An alternative may be to offer students a facility for emailing specific questions and to set aside specific times when these will be answered. If it seems likely that there will be too many to answer individually it may be possible to answer the questions in a block email for all the students in the module. In doing this, the module leader can develop a list of frequently asked questions (FAQs) that can be useful to subsequent cohorts. These questions will also give you feedback about your approach to teaching particular topics, which should help you avoid similar problems in the future. If there are many similar questions you may decide to respond by devoting time to them in a lecture or tutorial.

Optional resources

Conventional reading lists often seem to assume that all students learn best from reading and that a limited range of types of reading material is appropriate for all students. However, modules with a wide variety of students may benefit from visual material (e.g. Open University videos), audio material (e.g. audio-taped lectures), computer-based

In soils there are all these students from engineering, like a big gang. The lecturer goes to a lot of trouble to explain the background for them, but we've done all that before. I really think it lowers the standard we are working at.

materials (e.g. web documents, simulations, tutorials and self-testing material), and a much wider range of reference material than is normally suggested (e.g. text books, encyclopaedia entries, open learning self-teaching materials, lecturers' notes). Students will make use of such resources to varying extents depending on their different background knowledge, interests, needs and learning preferences.

Biological science for health science students using optional resources

This biological science module was designed for over 150 mature nursing and midwifery students, some of whom had no science background at all, or who failed science at school, and who needed science in order to be nurses rather than scientists. A range of support materials was created to accommodate different learning needs and styles. Given that these students have chosen to be carers and are interested in people, wherever possible the visual materials have a personal and medical focus and are aimed at showing relevance and stimulating interest.

The materials include:

- a huge bank of high quality colour OHPs;

- video extracts from Open University introductory science courses (used with their permission);

- extracts from the university's own archive of video interviews with famous medical scientists;

- introductory handouts provided for students to read before each lecture;

- partially completed handouts provided at each session, to which the students may add their own notes; and

- 'fast stream' literature available for those who already have much of the scientific knowledge, to allow them to progress further while maintaining a connection with the mainstream course.

The module also offers 'surgeries' for those who want to pursue problems arising from study materials.

'Graded' resources

Instead of specifying reading material for a module that assumes a uniform level of background knowledge and study histories, draw up 'graded' lists specifying that particular sources are introductory, intermediate or advanced in level. Suggest a sequence to work through and starting points for different levels of background knowledge or different study histories (e.g. 'If you have not taken module mnpq you are advised to start with X before moving on to Y').

> **A geomorphology module supported by graded study resources**
>
> An upper-level geomorphology module involved students from a wide range of physical geography, geology, biology and environmental science backgrounds. The module culminated in a group project that required all students to address a series of issues at the same advanced level. However, at the outset the variation in knowledge background and level was wide.
>
> After a four-week lecture and textbook-based introduction to bring students up to a similar level, project work was supported by a wide range of specially collated resource materials located in a resource centre in the department. Each of the main issues addressed in the module had its own files of background resources labelled with the level at which the material was dealt with and the background knowledge assumed. Files filling in background biology, geology and geomorphology information were also supplied. Introductory material, such as short videos or handbooks, were produced by groups of students from previous deliveries of the module, after they had understood the level and approach required. The range of files and their contents have been built up over a number of years in response to student needs as they have arisen.

Flexible module delivery

In most modular schemes, the majority of modules are designed on the assumption that students need the same content and learn at the same rate and at the same time. Indeed, the short duration of most modules and large numbers of students increases the pressure to attempt to move all students through the material at the same (fast) rate regardless of their varying needs. A lack of flexibility of some timetables for module delivery can exacerbate these problems for students with diverse backgrounds. Even Imperial College, with its comparatively well-qualified and homogeneous student body, is abandoning some science lecture programmes and replacing them with flexible resource-based courses to cope with student diversity.

Even in the most regimented programme structures, alongside the 'conventional modules' there are usually project, dissertation or independent learning modules, which by their very nature have to be designed on the assumption that it is the student who determines the appropriate rate of and therefore times for learning. It is worth investigating how far your particular institution's implementation of a modular scheme allows you to utilise some of the techniques used in these modules, to respond to the diverse needs of diverse students.

Alongside the pressure for coping with student diversity is the pressure for greater 'efficiency' which is leading to the development of new ways to deliver learning packages. Quite extensive investment is being made in computer systems and networks to provide learning materials in ways that are far more interactive than old-style computer-aided

I find it impossible to pitch my lectures at the right level. If I aim it at those without a science background our own students go to sleep or don't turn up and if I aim it at our own students the others just look blank.

learning (CAL) was ever able to be. Through the internet, students can access information from a range of sources and communicate with one another and with teaching staff through email, lists, online discussion groups or newsgroups.

It is beyond the scope of this book to consider resource-based learning (RBL) and online teaching and learning in any depth, but there is a section at the end of this chapter which introduces it.

Resources for flexible delivery

Some suggestions for adding flexibility to conventional modules are:

- use printed materials as substitutes for or supplements to lectures in order to avoid some of the difficulties of fixed pacing and timing associated with students with different knowledge backgrounds and timetables;

- use printed materials as briefing for labs, fieldwork, projects or other learning tasks where students may differ in their familiarity with learning processes, techniques, equipment etc.;

- use printed or RBL materials as 'remedial' support for students with specific gaps in their background or difficulties with topics; and

- use regular testing to identify to which resource materials or other remedial support to refer different students.

It is also possible to base modules very largely around learning materials, whether in learning packages or in special collections in the library, and to limit class contact to briefing students for individualised and self-paced independent work based on these materials, and to reviewing the work they do. Some such modules have come to resemble distance learning on campus. If they are intended as such then the student learners must be made aware of the greater self-motivation and discipline which is needed to be successful; otherwise there is a real risk that they will have a largely unsatisfactory learning experience. If, on the other hand, adequate student support is provided the approach can be very successful. Suitable student support includes study skills support, access to tutorial advice, regular feedback on progress and, for less mature and independent students, social support and a framework which provides some pacing.

Learning contracts

More extreme forms of flexibility include the use of learning contracts where students negotiate their own learning activities with their own personally relevant goals. Large enrolment modules with short time scales are not an ideal environment for such processes unless students have already become quite sophisticated independent learners. They are, however, increasingly being used for professional development. Individual or small group learning opportunities can be provided within a modular structure by defining the module as a 'shell' within which specified learning objectives or knowledge might be achieved by different students. Care must be taken in these situations to ensure that all students are treated in the same way and that learning stays within the accepted limits of the module specification.

Flexible first phase

It may be more effective simply to be flexible during the early phase of a module to bring students up to a common level from which they may progress together. In some science modules at the University of Nottingham a diagnostic test at the start is used to identify which of a range of perhaps four different short 'pre-units' each student might need to take, with the module proper not starting until week four and then progressing conventionally.

Checks on progress, with feedback

Even at Harvard University the students like short test questions during lectures because it gives them a good idea how they are doing and what they need to work on. Instead of trying to control students by testing them and allocating them to appropriate remedial provision it can be very effective to allow them to make their own decisions about what they should pay attention to – but to do this they need good, and frequent, information on their progress. Given appropriate self-test information and some minimal feedback most, though not all, students will make sensible decisions about their study needs, especially if clear options are made available. For example, a self-test can be accompanied by model answers and advice about where to find additional learning resources if the student judges that further studying is required. RBL techniques can be useful in this sort of situation even if they are not more widely used.

It is also possible to set a test and review just a proportion of the students' work, sampling several of each 'type' of student, and then giving general advice to each type at the next lecture. For example, in a science module taken by both biology and nursing students the feedback was:

From looking at these lab reports it seems as though the nursing students need to pay more attention to technical details such as labelling axes of graphs and specifying the units clearly, while the biology students need to pay more attention to their writing: paragraphs, grammar, spelling and coherent readable sentences.

Multiple layers of support

The level of support which some students will need is simply too extensive and expensive to provide for all students and also probably unnecessary. It may, however, be possible to provide a range of levels of support that is economical and efficient for a majority of able or well-prepared students and progressively more expensive forms of support for progressively smaller proportions of students with progressively greater needs. The example from the introductory physics module illustrates the way the use of multiple levels of support were provided to maintain overall performance on an introductory science module despite enormously increased numbers and diversity.

Video/audio lectures

Although many modules don't specify prerequisites, there are usually some background topics that students might have benefited from encountering before they start the module. If students arrive on a module through a variety of routes, each such topic is likely to have

---

An introductory physics module with multiple layers of support

An introduction to physics module at Oxford Brookes University gradually expanded until nearly 200 students with enormously varied knowledge and study backgrounds took the module. It would have been difficult to provide one-to-one or even small problem class support to cope with the varied needs of everybody and so a number of layers of support were provided instead.

Layer 1   consisted of a weekly overview lecture of which all students took advantage.

Layer 2   consisted of a study guide for a textbook that made appropriate assumptions about students' maths background. The study guide contained objectives, study guidance and self-test questions. All students used this layer but some needed to spend much more time with the textbook and guide than others.

Layer 3   consisted of a weekly multiple choice question test that was computer marked within 12 hours. Most, though not all, students took this test to see how they were getting on. It didn't contribute to module marks. Confident students could tell from the self-test questions in the guide that they had already mastered the week's topics. After the test about three-quarters of the students could see that either they had done enough for the week or that they could see what more they needed to do but didn't need help.

Layer 4   consisted of several different problem classes the day after the test. The lecturer selected various problems that students handled badly in the test to focus on in these sessions and about a quarter of students referred themselves to attend one or more of these sessions.

Layer 5   consisted of one-to-one individual tutorial slots of 10 minutes, bookable after the problem classes, if students still needed help. Only about 5% of students signed up for this layer of support, a quantity the lecturer could cope with.

---

been missed by some of them. These topics may well have been tackled in lectures in other modules. It is often only a few key lectures that are important rather than a whole module; otherwise the module would have been made a prerequisite. Audio- or video-recorded lectures can be used to make some of these topics easily available to students.

It is very easy to audio-record lectures and to place an audio-tape in the library for access on demand. It is less easy, though still not difficult, to video-record lectures, though only the most visual of lectures may benefit from the quality of visual prompts it is normally possible to record adequately. If only audio-recording is available it may be important to provide a set of copies of any overhead transparencies or other visual aids used in the lectures. The quality of recording does not have to be high: these lectures are supplementary material rather than key sources and are likely to be selectively sampled rather than listened to as a full lecture in any case.

If such recordings are undertaken on a routine basis a library of lectures can be built up over time. Key lectures from preceding modules can be identified for students who have not taken these modules, and they can listen to them in the library and compensate, to some extent, for not having taken the modules. These lectures can be listed alongside readings and brought to students' attention, e.g.:

> Lecture 3 assumes some familiarity with central place theory. Those without such familiarity are advised to read Jones, 1993, pages 74–81 and to listen to an audio-taped lecture by Professor Pepper entitled 'Central Place Theory and the Geography of Cities' (library reference 357.14).

The routine recording and cataloguing of lectures also helps those students who, for whatever reason, might have fallen behind or who have timetable clashes (if modules are allowed to be taken in such cases).

A related but somewhat easier-to-provide resource is to make a set of overhead transparencies from lectures available as PowerPoint (or similar) slides on the module or course web site together with associated lecture notes. (See also the section on resource-based learning below.)

Mixing students

For environmental science field trips at Oxford Brookes University, groups are deliberately formed from students who take a variety of other subjects along with environmental science. Each group ends up with a mixture of geologists, geographers, biologists and so on, bringing a wide range of expertise and perspectives to the field trip. In the example from hotel and catering management the selection of students within project groups is even more carefully arranged.

Hotel and catering management – creating balanced groups for a project assignment

A 3rd-year module with between 100 and 200 students includes a major project involving the preparation of plans to develop a hotel or conference facility in a 'green field' site. The students vary greatly in their background, which could cause considerable difficulties if the project groups of 7–10 students were too unbalanced in their membership.

The module leader uses a class list and spreadsheet to create groups that reflect the variety of students. Ideally the groups have a balance of gender; of UK, European and Far Eastern students; of students who study hotel and catering management as their main or only as their subsidiary subject; and of students who have followed different specialist pathways within the degree. The final addition to the mix comes from a consultation with the module leader responsible for previous modules on financial management, who identifies students with high grades and ability and allocates one of these students to each project group.

Specialised modules

Modularisation has often been used as a way of rationalising the use of resources by combining into one module the content and outcomes of a number of similar modules offered to students on different programmes. For example, all students who need some law may be put together in one large and, supposedly, cost-effective introduction to law module. The problems caused by the diversity of interest, motivation and background knowledge of students in such modules have sometimes been overwhelming and led to expensive remedial attention, low retention and failure. These 'expenses' seem usually to be ignored when cost-effective solutions are discussed.

One solution to such problems, however, has seen departments exerting pressure so that a broad-based module is broken up again into several parallel modules, each with a separate specialist focus or approach to similar material. For example, a 'law for management' module or even a 'law for hotel and catering management' module may be provided. Arguments in favour of doing this suggest that law students will be less likely to be held back by less committed or less advanced management students, who will be provided with more relevant management law content.

The main course delivery costs for very large enrolment modules are often associated with running seminars rather than with lectures. The additional costs of new lectures on such parallel modules may be relatively modest, and probably lower than costs associated with the necessary remedial support and high failure rates common with very large generalist modules. On the other hand, an insistence that introductory modules must be subject specific can often arise from

We put students together in two different ways: in their seminars they are with others from the same background but in their projects they work in 'interdisciplinary' groups. I think it exploits their differences well.

simple academic 'tribalism' or because module leaders want to continue what they were doing before modularisation.

In psychology it has become common for popular introductory modules to be offered in two forms: one involving laboratory and scientific content for students going on to seek British Psychological Society recognition, and one more economical and less technical for non-psychology students (who are in the great majority). This is both cheaper and more effective than putting all students through the same module, though it can result in the generalist version of the module being categorised as 'non-science' and being funded accordingly.

Specialist seminar groups

An alternative approach to tackling the problems of generalist modules is to leave the lectures common for all subgroups of students but to have the small group sessions, whether seminars or problem classes, run by tutors from the subject areas the students come from. The example from an introduction to statistics module adopted this approach. If it is

---

Student diversity on an introduction to chemistry module – evaluating problems and supporting students

As student numbers increased on this chemistry module, so too did the problem of diversity. There were growing numbers of students with no chemistry background, some of whom took the module as a prerequisite for courses such as geology. The module involves lectures for large numbers, practical sessions scattered throughout the week for smaller numbers and optional surgeries. Three major problems were identified:

- some students had insufficient previous knowledge of or ability in mathematics;

- many students felt 'lost in a crowd'; and

- 'surgery' sessions were dominated by discussion on how to write up practicals.

Changes made to overcome these problems included:

- the production of a remedial mathematics package for students to work through as and when they feel appropriate;

- a reduction in the mathematics content to what was essential (more advanced mathematics being tackled in later modules, for those who continued with chemistry);

- changes in the syllabus to focus on areas more relevant to students from outside chemistry, such as geologists, wherever possible;

- changes in the practical groups to establish greater identity and better social relationships, including keeping the same demonstrator for the whole module; and

- scrapping the writing up of practicals as an assessment task, freeing up surgery time for problems with the subject matter (practical report writing being tackled in later modules, for those who continued with chemistry).

Subject-specific problem classes on a statistics module

An introduction to statistics module with a huge enrolment and taught by a statistics department had all the problems one would expect for students from psychology, town planning, sociology, biology and so on, subjects in which statistical methods are applied in different ways to different kinds of data. To avoid each subject area abandoning the generic 'Introduction to Statistics' module and offering their own discipline-specific versions, the module was redesigned.

A statistics lecturer continued to give the lectures and to teach students how to use a statistics computer package. The weekly problem classes were run by tutors from students' own subject areas. A psychology tutor, for example, would devise problems involving the application of that week's statistical methods to psychological data and handle the classes for all the psychology students. All coursework assignments and exam questions were subject specific, being variations on questions set by the statistician.

---

logistically impossible to arrange subject-specific tutors another approach would be to devise subject-specific problems and to allocate students to subject-specific problem classes tutored by a statistician.

Varied assignments

Where the subject 'source' of students can be identified it is possible to design essay questions, problems or other forms of assignment which relate to each of these subject areas. Students can then select an assignment which, while addressing the same generic issues or using the same techniques as all other parallel assignments, is based in a context of personal relevance. Tutors from these 'source' subjects can be asked to devise subject-specific variants of generic questions or problems, for example by setting case study contexts.

Graded assignments

In maths and engineering it is common to use problem sheets which contain a list of problems that are progressively more difficult and advanced. Students work through the list as far as they can manage. The same general notion can be extended to a variety of topics. All students would be expected to be able to tackle certain problems or tasks or demonstrate certain competencies but the more difficult problems would challenge advanced students. What distinguishes students' marks on such a module might not be simply how well they tackled assignments but also the level of sophistication of the assignments the students chose to tackle. Students needing only to pass a particular module could tackle the easier assignments or questions confident that success in these would lead to a pass while those wanting high marks or to cover as much material as possible could tackle more advanced assignments.

Alternative assignments in an accountancy module

The leader of an accountancy module at the University of East London had a wide variety of mature students with different ethnic and educational backgrounds (Bashir, 1994). Print-based resources and video-taped lectures were developed. Students were able to choose three of six optional units within the module, and drew on these resources for their learning. They could take tests on their choice of two out of their three optional units and choose when to take these tests. Students were also allowed to choose between alternative forms of tests for the units. The end of module examination remained the same. The failure rate dropped from 75% to 25%.

It is of course important that the 'pass' level still reflects the achievement of the threshold level for the learning outcomes specified for the module – a matter which needs to be addressed when the module is designed rather than when it is delivered. (See Part 1 for more on threshold levels.)

Specialised reading lists

Where there are identifiable subgroups of students from different subject areas it may be possible to identify literature that applies the theories or methods addressed in a module to those subject areas. The range of suitable literature available may, for example:

- examine questionnaire design in psychology, sociology or marketing;

- describe the customisation of computer spreadsheets to a variety of subject-based contexts;

- apply general systems theory to a variety of physical phenomena based in different sciences; or

- apply basic theory to a specific profession, such as social psychology theory to social work or management theory to engineering businesses.

It may also be possible to use literature of completely different types and genres to suit particular subgroups. For example, novels that explore psychological phenomena may be used in conjunction with conventional textbooks to help English students studying psychology. Collaborating with module leaders and tutors in the relevant subject areas is important for identifying suitable texts. 'Fast stream' literature can be made available for confident students wishing to progress to more advanced material in later modules.

Resource-based learning

It is no coincidence that the recent rapid expansion in the use of resource-based learning (RBL) materials, particularly computer software and world wide web based materials, together with the flexible forms of course delivery they allow, has accompanied the spread of modularisation. There is concern in some quarters that moving from 'conventional classes' for teaching to other techniques and technologies will actually undermine the quality of HE. There is a growing body of evidence and practice that shows that these techniques can successfully be used both to supplement more traditional modes of module delivery and to deliver complete modules.

Course design for resource-based learning project

The HEFCE funded 'Course design for resource-based learning' project identified and collated a variety of ways in which different subject areas have exploited the flexibility resource-based learning offers. The project produced a series of publications in 1994 (Gibbs, 1994) that document case studies and analyse key module design issues.

Since this project was completed, much more work has been done and most Higher Education Institutes (HEI) have sought to promote RBL as one way to teach more students at less cost, and to provide appropriate support for 'distance learning'. Online learning, which includes the provision of RBL materials via the world wide web, is a more recent variation on these methods. Despite the obvious success of many distance learning programmes, there are still some who disparage the whole idea that students can learn without interacting personally with a tutor or lecturer and on these grounds try to dismiss completely the use of RBL. This approach is short sighted and fails to understand that we need to know which topics, skills, techniques, knowledge and ideas are best taught in which particular ways.

The American Association for Higher Education has created a forum for discussion, debate and shared good practice through its newsgroup AAHESGIT, which has recently been changed to TLT-SWG. Archives may be consulted at the url:

www.cren.net:8080/guest/archives/AAHESGIT or
www.cren.net:8080/guest/archives/TLT-SWG/.

RBL, online learning and distance learning are all subjects for discussion. Commenting in the introduction on a piece by Ehrmann (2000), Steve Gilbert, the AAHESGIT editor, wrote of the importance of:

> learning how to use the unique characteristics, dimensions, and possibilities of face-to-face communications as well as new telecommunications options

and claims that means:

> we need to learn much more about the important dimensions of human communication... to avoid the reductionist trap of assuming that capturing any one dimension (e.g. the words) is capturing everything.

According to AAHESGIT-60, the potential advantages of online learning include:

- **convenience**: anytime, anywhere;

- **immediacy**: students receive speedier feedback on assignments;

- **contact**: more instructor/student contact and peer-to-peer contact;

- **learner control**: students can have more say in what or how they learn;

- **technology**: students and teachers gain greater proficiency with the internet and other tools for finding, using, and constructing information;

- **prestige**: online programmes carry a cutting-edge cachet; and

- **new learning**: students and professors can construct new knowledge in ways they couldn't without the technology.

Potential disadvantages of online learning include:

- **facelessness**: lack of verbal and facial cues, body language;

- **glitches**: technological breakdowns;

- **workload**: much more work to develop, produce, teach, and take an online course;

- **cost**: courses with audio, video, interactivity, etc., cost more to produce;

- **support**: finding 24/7 technical support; offering professors incentives to produce and teach online; revising a tenure system that discounts online teaching; revamping or building registration, enrolment, and payment methods; deciding where online courses will 'fit', (integrate into every department? 'spin off' an online unit? partner with outside institution?); and

- **quality**: new methods required for accreditation and measuring 'outcomes'.

Oxford Brookes University Web Course Tools

In January 2001, Brookes introduced WebCT, a web-based online (or virtual) learning environment (VLE), to enhance its teaching and learning. It allows provision of information and resources relating to a module, and might include course details, lecture notes, assignments, online discussions, quizzes and more. Online learning is primarily focused on enhanced communications and access to learning resources, rather than providing an electronic textbook. It is also accessible off campus, indeed from anywhere that a student has access to the internet.

On the Homepage there are links to:

- the Course Facilities page, the main navigation area within WebCT which includes links to all of the course tools;

- the Content area, which may present a structured list of the main course materials, such as documents, lecture notes, presentations and diagrams;

- the Discussions forum, which can host discussions on particular topics defined by the module leader – students can post and reply to messages, search, compile and print them; and

- an Announcements area.

Other 'tools' relevant to the 'coping with student diversity' theme allow students to:

- search the course content and discussion forums for any word or phrase;

- discuss topics in real-time or asynchronously with other students and tutors;

- take part in online tests that can be marked automatically with instant feedback, for formative or summative assessment; and

- view assignment requirements, download related material, and upload assignment files for marking.

Virtual learning environments similar to WebCT are being adopted by HEIs around the UK and internationally, for both distance and on-campus course provision. Evaluations of the delivery software, course materials provided, their impact on student learning and demands on staff time are ongoing. The important point is that as HEIs recognise the value of such tools and assist teaching staff by making them readily available and easily useable, module leaders seeking to cope with diversity will add ways of using the web for teaching and learning to their skills.

Using the web to help cope with student diversity

The web also allows new variations on some techniques described earlier. A variant of video/audio lectures allows streamed synchronised slides, video and/or audio to be delivered via the web as either prerecorded or 'live' events. These are most likely to be an effective way

Fig. 6.1: Oxford Brookes University Web Course Tools

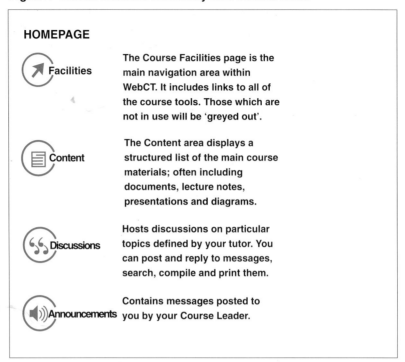

HOMEPAGE

Facilities — The Course Facilities page is the main navigation area within WebCT. It includes links to all of the course tools. Those which are not in use will be 'greyed out'.

Content — The Content area displays a structured list of the main course materials; often including documents, lecture notes, presentations and diagrams.

Discussions — Hosts discussions on particular topics defined by your tutor. You can post and reply to messages, search, compile and print them.

Announcements — Contains messages posted to you by your Course Leader.

to deal with student diversity when other facets, such as multisite delivery, support for independent learning, or an optional resource are exploited simultaneously. An example of such technology is 'Horizonlive' (www.horizonlive.com) used in conjunction with Blackboard (2002), a content management system for internet-enhanced learning. Boxmind (www.boxmind.com) is another similar technology.

Another variation that requires little technical skill but good teaching expertise is use of discussion forums as an addition to or replacement for seminar groups. Discussion forums used together with student presentation areas also allow for sophisticated group work among students, developing key skills in areas of communications, technology and team work as well as expertise in the subject area. Composing groups with diverse backgrounds can enhance group work, as discussed earlier. Students with common subject backgrounds can be grouped together as necessary, while retaining common access to course materials. Web-based teaching and learning innovations appear to hold great promise for coping with student diversity.

Pretests and self-tests on progress using multiple choice questions can be provided on the web or on paper for students. Wrong answers to questions can be linked to resources that provide the student with explanations or references to other materials. Optional materials and 'graded resources' can be provided from even a single web page with links to other web pages, enriching resources available for students from diverse academic backgrounds. As the web gives access to a wealth of such resources, providing links to already existing material, especially together with annotations about the quality of each site, is generally better use of module leaders' time than writing one's own resource materials.

Promoting learning through student interaction

Barbara Millis (2001), Director of the Faculty Development Center for Educational Excellence at the US Air Force Academy, wrote, quoting Rhem (source unknown), that to promote learning through online activities we should:

> encourage the kind of student interactions and active learning that foster deep learning ... assignments should motivate students to learn ... they should build on a carefully structured, integrated knowledge base .... Learning should include active student involvement and interaction among students. ... Effective, creative uses of technology should rest on all we know about human learning. Not surprisingly, the same principles – that foster effective in-class learning, can also promote learning at a distance.

She goes on to list 17 principles, some of which (e.g. 'aim for heterogeneous groups' and 'to ensure heterogeneity, form teams') have been described earlier in this chapter as practical ways of dealing with student diversity.

Supporting independent learning through a web-based discussion forum

At the University of Reading, a corporate real estate and facilities management MSc module begins with two days in residence and then continues for four weeks using a web-based discussion forum. Individual students are given responsibility for raising a question for discussion and 'posting' some comments and observations. Other students then join in by reading what has been written and posting their own response. The discussions can be followed and joined whenever and wherever a student wishes because each topic is identified as a separate 'thread' and listed in an index.

The particular application to student diversity is that any student can start a new thread or follow and participate in an existing one. The module leader can respond to threads by providing answers or asking questions that are available to all students in the forum and not just a group that are in the same place at the same time. Where there are large numbers of students on a module, it is better to split them into a number of separate forums to avoid overloading the discussion.

Perhaps a very useful point to remember from such an experienced practitioner is:

> No matter how carefully you plan, some things will invariably go wrong. Don't despair: numerous educators have emphasised the value of risk-taking to professional growth. The point is not to give up ('Oh, I tried online group work and it didn't work at all'). Seek help from knowledgeable colleagues and from faculty development centres where you will find books, articles, and professionals who can offer indirect advice or who can observe your online classes.

Supporting students with visual or hearing impairment

Although the diverse backgrounds and experiences of students with disabilities are not the main features of 'student diversity' discussed in this chapter, it is appropriate, in the context of RBL, to mention some of the facilities that are available to support learning undertaken by students with particular disabilities. Firstly, for complete accessibility to online materials, web sites should meet the World Wide Web Consortium (W3C) Web Accessibility Standards (WAI, 2001). For example, navigation around a site should not be only graphical. Seminars using discussion forums are a good way to be inclusive (as long as the technology is WAI compliant), assisting both visual and hearing impaired students simultaneously. The RNIB (2001a) 'See it

---

Assistive technology for a registered blind student

The RNIB (2001b) advises that a visually impaired student who is confident using a computer and screen reader, and who has technical support from friends and the RNIB when required, could use the following technology and assistance to handle web-based learning tasks:

- a computer screen reader for internet pages and digital documents – screen readers can read aloud any accessible text, whether web pages or documents, displayed on-screen using a normal computer;

- a stand-alone scanner for hardcopy documents of 1–5 pages – this device can work either with a computer running suitable software, or as a portable audio reading assistant; longer documents are more difficult to manage with this equipment because of the time taken to scan each page for screen reader access (journals with columns cannot be read easily with a scanner and screen reader);

- Braille reading for hardcopy documents of 5–10 pages – if a student reads Braille at 30–40 words per minute, documents of this length are preferable in Braille; and

- a personal reader, and/or RNIB transcription to audio service, for long documents.

right' campaign gives useful information about a range of resources, e.g. video used in presentations.

Presentations using 'PowerPoint' or whiteboards are no use to visually impaired students. It is preferable to give these students access to a copy as a text file via email, disc, CD (but be aware of compatibility issues), HTML web page, or PDF file (with accessible plug-in). If possible, provide this before the lecture so that the student is not disadvantaged and can keep up to speed during the presentation.

Summary points

As a module leader wanting to cope with student diversity it is important to:

- identify the needs of students who have different prior learning and provide suitable support so they can start from a common level;

- make sure that each small group has either a similar 'mix' of students or students from a single background, depending on the purpose and nature of the assignment the group is required to complete;

- consider giving students on different programmes different assignments to assess the same learning outcomes; and

- consider to what extent RBL can be an effective means of achieving some of these aims.

Managing marking and maintaining feedback

7

This chapter reviews problems commonly associated with marking and feedback in modular programmes. It explores ways to structure assessment in modular schemes, and the use of clear criteria to enhance both marking and feedback. Finally, it suggests ways that marking and feedback time can be reduced while improving student learning, through varying assessment types and using peer and self assessment effectively.

Assessment in modular schemes

Increased marking loads for tutors and increased examination and coursework loads for students are perhaps the most common and bitter complaints about modularisation. Although module teams may be able to agree on criteria for marking particular assignments, there is no general agreement as to how honours degrees within a modular scheme should be classified. Nationally, however, there is no general agreement as to what should constitute degree classification. Should it relate to the standard achieved by a student at the end of their course? Should it be a measure of a student's average performance in their last stage (or year)? Should the classification relate to a student's weighted average performance over a longer period – the last stages (or years) of their course?

At the time of writing it does not seem likely that any decisions about this will be made by the QAA in the near future although it does state (QAA, 2000, p. 10) that:

> Institutions should publish clear criteria for the aggregation of marks and grades and the rules and regulatuions for progression, final awards and classifications.

Consequently the minimum amount of assessment required for honours classification and the time period over which it should be carried out is not universally agreed. In modular schemes the classification algorithm gives largest weight to modules passed in the final stage of an honours programme. Research into student performance at Oxford Brookes University (Lindsay et al, 1998) showed clearly that students' marks on modules improved term on term and were usually dependent on the number of modules being studied contemporaneously.

Some schemes use a profile and others an average; it may also be compulsory to include the results obtained on particular modules. It is commonly found that whichever system is used about ten per cent of students results will be in the borderline area, i.e. if they had obtained a few marks more or less on say one module, then their degree classification would have been different (SACWG, 1997). In these cases using a different method to calculate the class may give a different result.

Transcripts of performance

Apart from honours classification, most schemes issue successful students with a transcript which specifies their performance in each module. This is usually seen by both students and university authorities as 'a good thing', valued by employers and a useful addendum to a CV. It is therefore unfortunate, to say the least, to find that most formal assessments are extraordinarily unreliable! For example, a study at Cambridge University (Laming, 1990) found no significant correlations between any pairs of first and second markers of essays: marks were effectively random! Such findings are the norm rather than the exception and are in part caused by the sheer volume of marking which prevents tutors from spending enough time to mark reliably. Of course no individual likes to believe that their assessments are without value and most would be able to cite results of assessment by second markers (whether internal or external) which correlated well with their own, as evidence to counter the studies mentioned.

Using criteria to mark essays

One good result of these publicised uncertainties has been the increase in specification of the criteria used in assessing assignments. Indeed QAA (2001, p. 9) expect that 'Institutions should publish, and implement consistently, clear criterea for the marking and grading of assessments.' Gosling and Moon (2001) have useful advice on developing criteria which are essential if more than one person is assessing on a given module. It also helps students understand how the assessment 'works', and may therefore, as a side effect, enable them to improve their performance. When module leaders also run a workshop with their co-assessors to check how they operationalise the criteria and the performance specifications, there is increased expectation of consistency and reproducibility. Among other points of practice that should be considered are the use of second marking, the reliability of sampling methods from larger groups, maintaining an archive of sample marked scripts ans analysis of trends in results (op.cit.). Workshops designed to help students explore and understand the criteria can also lead to better student work (Price & Rust, 2001).

Too much assessment?

For a modular programme, as opposed to one which is taught as a set of units, each module carries with it a certain volume of credit and consequently each module must be assessed. This generally means there must be at least one piece of assessed work per module, which is capable of giving information about whether a student has achieved the minimum learning outcomes specified for the module. In some schemes some modules may be assessed as pass/fail and not otherwise graded. All this is a far cry from three-year linear programmes which classified students on the results of, say, six exam papers, taken towards the end of the three years. There would seem to be little doubt that compared with that linear structure, a modular scheme requires:

- students to spend more time on preparing assignments for assessment; and

- module leaders to spend more time on marking assignments.

This has led to the general perception that in modular schemes there is too much assessment and the naive assumption that if the amount of assessment was drastically reduced, students could spend more time on learning and staff could spend more time on teaching. As has already been noted, assessment has apparently become one of the currencies of volume of credit. Students may like the idea that they could gain a 'credit' in one module by submitting very little work for assessment, but will claim it is unfair if in another they are required to spend more time on assessed work!

Students' time is competed for by the different modules they take and as the overall workload cannot easily be planned in modular courses this competition sometimes becomes fierce. A module with a series of weekly assessed components such as lab reports or problem sheets will capture more student time than a module with a single essay that isn't due until week 10. Those designing modules have learnt to set early and frequent deadlines. Bear in mind, however, that students' evaluation feedback about their perceived workloads rarely correspond to their actual workloads. With increasing financial pressures leading to more students with part-time jobs, perhaps the majority of students are not putting in a full studying week. Demands from students for less assessed work need to be interpreted with care.

All the assignments from my modules have to be in in the same week, often on the same day, and the modules are so short there isn't time to fit it all in so you end up skimping. There is no coordination of deadlines at all.

The role of feedback in learning

The simplest way of reducing assessment is to mark students' work considerably less often. But this, of course, overlooks those functions of assessment which support learning:

- assessed tasks capture students' time and effort;

- assignments can generate appropriate types of learning activity; and

- marking and commenting on work can provide feedback to guide students in their learning.

An assessed essay generates a particular kind of reading around to put extended arguments together. This form of reading is quite different from that engaged in to prepare for seminars or to follow up lectures. Take the essay away and this form of reading simply disappears and with it the learning it produces. Introducing multiple choice questions because they are economical and can give at least minimal feedback quickly will achieve little if it results in students taking a surface approach and simply memorising facts instead of trying to understand ideas or tackle complex problems.

While feedback is crucial to learning, the feedback many students get is less than ideal even where work is marked regularly. Where student numbers are high and time is short, work often receives only superficial attention and feedback is limited in value. It also often comes late: certainly too late to influence the way students study the topic of the assignment or how they present their understanding of the topic. Where the main assignment deadline is towards the end of the module, as is usual, it is common for students not to receive feedback until after they have completed the module when it is really water under the bridge. And of course students rarely receive feedback on exam performance.

Part of the problem of giving feedback is that it is associated with marks and so great care has to be taken that there is no inconsistency between marks and comments which could lead to queries or appeals. This can lead to cautious and minimal comments. Despite the perceived volume of assessment the quality, timeliness and value of feedback is rarely as good as it might be. Students may be criticised for saying that they only care about the mark but this is at least in part because the feedback they receive is of so little help or relevance.

Whether students actually spend their time as planned should be a matter for evaluation: this is surely a more important evaluation issue than most normally addressed concerning lecturers' performance. Whether assignments, exams in particular, generate appropriate learning effort seems, for example, a particularly important question. Chapter 8 has more on evaluation.

Balancing feedback, learning and the volume of assessment

Applying explicit criteria with care and consistency to produce reliable results requires time and may delay feedback. Processes for sample double marking and external assessing must normally follow first marking and this means feedback is further delayed. Feedback may need to be qualitative in the first instance to avoid publication of unconfirmed results. Most systems only insist on sampling by an external examiner when the assignment makes a major contribution to the assessment of a module. This is helpful since it means final marks on, say, a presentation may be fed back quite quickly. However the volume of assessment needs to be limited if the institution's own standards are to be assured. If sufficient care is not taken over assessment in module design, module leaders will find that it is simply not possible to undertake properly the volume of marking that is generated. General requirements and standards of the assessment system are explained in Part 1.

Strategies for improving learning and reducing marking

The requirements of a sound assessment system may seem contradictory and even impossible within current resource constraints, and within short modules, but the following suggestions all meet at least several of these requirements. Some obviously lead to less marking; others may lead to better learning activities and make better use of students' time but not reduce the marking load. For more extended accounts of these methods, see Gibbs (1992, 1995a).

'Required' tasks

Students can be required to undertake various tasks and provide evidence that they have done so without staff having to 'mark' these or even give feedback on them. This practice is usually intended to guarantee that students engage in crucial learning activities. Even though the work is not given a specific mark or grade, care must be taken to check it has been submitted, that it is complete and that it is genuine. It is not unknown for the occasional student to steal, plagiarise, or manufacture the evidence. Examples of such course requirements can include:

- attendance on field trips;

- submission of laboratory notebooks as evidence of having undertaken laboratory work;

- submission of a variety of written work such as a book review, an annotated bibliography, a short essay;

- submission of a log book detailing practical work undertaken in architecture, performances listened to in music, museum and gallery visits in art history, work experiences in nursing; or

- submission of accounts of seminars, detailing prior reading.

Such requirements can be made prerequisites for passing the course or for sitting exams. Feedback can be provided in other ways, which will be discussed in the next few pages. Requirements need to be completely explicit and unambiguous, for example:

> Your laboratory notebook must contain complete reports, including interpretation of data, on at least eight of the ten laboratory sessions, each signed by the demonstrator involved.

Another way of making the tasks 'required' is to relate them to a separate item of assessment which follows some time later in the module. In an introductory chemistry module at Oxford Brookes, there were students with a wide variety of backgrounds in chemistry. The module leader looked for a way in which he could encourage students

---

Formative testing – use of web-based multiple-choice questions

Software designed to create simple web-based multiple choice tests that gave instant feedback was used. For each week's work of the introductory chemistry module, a set of practice questions was created to form a formative web-based assessment. These practice tests were available from the very start of the module. The students could attempt them in their own time, gaining instant feedback on how well they had understood that week's topic.

In order to persuade students (other than the very enthusiastic ones) to use the practice tests, the students were told that five out of the 20 questions set each week would appear on the final exam. With eight of these weekly tests available, this gave assiduous students the chance to try no fewer than 40 of the 80 final exam questions prior to the exam, although they had to do all 160 practice questions to achieve this.

The students were also told at the outset that some form of negative marking would be applied in the exam as the quid pro quo for half the exam being 'seen' and the possibility of gaining some marks by guess work.

---

to actively engage with the descriptive parts of chemistry (Grebenik & Rust, 2002). This also links back to the section on RBL in Chapter 6.

Negative marking is controversial; in this case it led to two unexpected consequences. Compared to the previous year, 'good' students or those who had worked hard on the practice tests got higher scores in the exam, while 'poor' or less committed students scored less well, due to negative marking. This was reflected in a 50% increase in the standard deviation on the exam mark. A further benefit from negative marking came from examining those questions that many students had chosen not to attempt. These indicated areas of the course in which students had developed little confidence, and that therefore needed to be taught differently.

Overall, these results suggest that strategic use of 'required' tasks, administered through a suitable computer application, can both reduce staff workload (ignoring the development overhead) and increase student learning. In particular, these applications have motivated and enabled students to structure work in their own time, and permitted them to make repeated efforts to get work right in an anonymous risk-free environment where initial wrong answers will not show them up in front of their peers or teachers.

Portfolios

Portfolios are collections of work submitted at the end of a period of study but collated throughout the study period, revealing the studying as it progressed. The archetypal example is an architecture portfolio in which students not only present a design but the design studies, background research sketches and so on which led to the final design. This is likely to cover around two thirds of a normal year of full-time study which could be between four and eight modules in most schemes. If the scheme allows for multicredit modules then good use can be made of the portfolio.

If the modular scheme doesn't allow for multicredit modules, sections of a portfolio could be resubmitted in different modules. General assessment regulations would have to make clear whether material submitted for one module that was not passed could be used in another.

A parallel process is possible in text-based subjects where the range of study activities leading to an exam performance or final project submission can be presented in a portfolio. Possible items for inclusion may be:

- reflections on reading, say, four books and four articles;

- preparation notes for four seminars;

- reflective notes on four (different) seminars;

- reflections and evidence of reading following four lectures;

- one seminar paper which was presented;

- one book review; and

- an annotated bibliography on one topic other than an essay topic.

There may simply be a requirement to submit such a portfolio, it may be used to moderate judgements of a project report or extended essay, or elements of the portfolio may be sampled for marking.

Sampling for marking

It may not be necessary to mark every piece of student work either to allocate a fair mark for the module or to produce serious attention from the student. For example it is possible to require engineering students to produce six lab reports but to mark only three of them, chosen at random. If there are a number of criteria by which each piece of work in the set could be marked, it is possible to sample criteria used in marking rather than mark using every criteria every time. One of the three lab reports could be marked for engineering content, one for handling and interpretation of data and one for written communication skills, ignoring the other criteria each time. If students do not know which reports are going to be assessed with which criteria, then they have to pay equal attention to every criterion every time. As the module progresses other feedback mechanisms such as model answers, peer feedback and sampling for feedback can be used. To make sure students do not improve and resubmit their reports after feedback has been provided, use an office date stamp on each page on the day of original submission.

Of course, this method isn't limited to engineering. Students in other discipline areas could be required to submit three short essays without knowing which one will be given a mark, or three designs, three case studies, three problem sheets, etc.

Sampling for feedback

In some assignments, typically lab reports and problem sheets, there is a limited range of approaches and thus of possible major errors or misunderstandings. Tutors will generally have noted the possible range of feedback comments long before completing the marking of a large pile of scripts. It may be possible to stop marking after seeing the first ten, then sampling a few others to seek out further variation. A summary of most feedback comments can probably be made without having seen more than a small sample of the scripts.

This feedback can then be written down and distributed as a handout or email, or presented to students in an oral summary at the next lecture or practical class. It may be useful for students to be asked to review their assignment to see which of the comments apply – doing this may even produce more reflection from students than conventional commenting on every script.

One interesting way to provide feedback to large numbers of students has been used for an introductory chemistry course involving the use of spreadsheets (Grebenik & Rust, 2002).

Use of feedback to encourage students to tackle numerical problems

For an introductory chemistry course at Oxford Brookes there was concern that students were not tackling numerical problems. To ensure that students did tackle these problems, and to help them become competent, questions were set up in an Excel spreadsheet. Students could enter their answers and be informed automatically whether the answer was correct. Students had to attempt six questions on each of five question types but were allowed to have as many attempts as they wanted, making it possible for them to get full marks if they persevered. There was also a second and more difficult set of questions in a second spreadsheet to increase the spread of marks and 'stretch' the better students.

To encourage student participation, a total of 15% of the overall module assessment was allocated to the two sets of problems. Students had to get a minimum mark of 30% on the combined spreadsheets. Otherwise they would automatically fail the module even if they scored well on the exam.

In another innovation in this module, a 'surgery' system was established for those students who needed extra help. The surgeries replaced small group problem classes that had not proven very satisfactory.

A very user friendly method by which the students downloaded their own spreadsheet from the school intranet was used. The spreadsheet was programmed so that each time it was saved to disk, it wrote a summary of student performance to a remote file. Although students found the second set of problems quite demanding (average mark of 56% compared to an average mark of 91% on the easier problem set), student evaluations of the spreadsheet problems was very positive. This approach had solved the problem of making students tackle simple numerical problems, and it gave them both instant feedback and some reward for their efforts.

In the evaluation of the module, most students reported the spreadsheet activity as one of the best things in it! Although not many students had attended the surgeries, the sessions were considered useful for those who needed them. Substantial savings in staff time were made by replacing the large number of relatively ineffective small group sessions with the surgeries.

Group assignments

It may take twice as long to give feedback on a group report produced by six students cooperatively as on an individual report, but it won't take six times as long. Feedback as a part of supervision of extended group project work is both economical and advantageous to student learning. Group work also encourages informal peer feedback as part of the group process. There is usually either less for tutors to have to comment on in group reports (because students have sorted more of the faults before submission) or the tutor can concentrate on more advanced issues in feedback.

Mechanisms for setting up groups, devising group assignments and allocating marks fairly to individuals within groups can be found in Gibbs (1995d).

Model answers

It is common in parts of maths and science where there are either 'right' answers, or at least only limited variations on best possible answers, to use 'model answers' as a way of giving feedback. The further you move from technical content to more open-ended studies that allow widely diverging solutions and analyses of issues, the less useful such model answers can become, to the point where they misleadingly suggest that there are 'right' answers. But model answers are more useful than no feedback at all, over quite a wide range of tasks and topics.

Model answers can be particularly useful for lab reports, fieldwork reports, case studies, interpretations of data and evidence, and reviews of books or fields of literature. Highlighting generic features of model answers, such as use of writing conventions and citation, appropriate uses of evidence, construction of argument, awareness of alternative theoretical perspectives etc., can be useful even for essay questions in which there is clearly no 'right' response.

Model answers with associated marks, grades or tutor comments can guide students towards the general standard to be aimed at, illustrate assessment criteria in use and calibrate self- and peer-assessment judgements to be in line with tutor judgements.

Peer assessment

Hinett and Thomas (1999) offer sceptics a tentative list of incentives for considering self- and peer-assessment practice:

- it focuses the time available for feedback on the substantive issues of theory and practice;

- it provides a structure and a framework for discussions about the quality of work;

- it enables students to plan for the future and to make changes to their work and practice while they are engaged in the process and act of learning;

- it helps students to become critical about their own work and the discipline-related body of knowledge;

- it helps students (particularly those in creative areas such as art, fashion or design) to understand that judgements about quality are subjective and can only be substantiated by reference to other work;

- it improves communication about quality and standards between students and staff; and

- it can be used as evidence of standards for the purpose of external accountability.

Module leaders may be familiar with peer assessment of group work, but may be less aware of its use in other contexts, for example the assessment of presentations. In these cases the marks awarded actually contribute in some way to the overall mark for the module. In group work students may assess one another's contributions to each element of a criteria list, such as background research, data collection, design ideas, etc. Module leaders can develop a set of clear criteria and rating scales and discuss these with the students before an assignment begins. Alternatively, students can be involved in developing criteria for assessing their work. Students may not have the experience to judge how good each team member is in absolute terms, but they are in a good position to tell whether their contributions were above or below average.

Peer assessment using model answers for 'required' problems

On a large second-year mechanical engineering course students were expected to undertake a substantial number of problems on tutorial sheets on a regular basis. However, many students did not undertake the problems or attend the tutorials. As a result the mid-term examinations revealed very poor performance and the end-of-course exam results were still poor. The two exams involved a substantial marking load but this marking failed to elicit appropriate learning behaviour and led to poor performance.

In the redesigned course students were required to complete 60 problems. Each of six units of work was accompanied by a series of tutorial problems and a tutor-marked 'degree standard' problem which had to be completed by a set date. Late submission of solutions was severely penalised. At the end of each unit students marked another's work in class as the tutor worked through correct solutions on the board using a standard 'marking solution' of which all students were given a copy.

Students' mid-term exam score increased markedly, with almost no failures. Almost all students completed sufficient problems successfully. Through the requirement to complete work, regular feedback and analysis of requirements, and provision of correct solutions, students changed their study habits and this produced improved performance on conventional, tutor-marked assessments. There is no need in such circumstances to have elaborate control over students' marking behaviour or checks on their reliability (Gibbs, 1995b).

Peer assessment and feedback in law

First-year law students were asked to prepare a detailed plan of their first written course assignment and bring it to their next learning set meeting two weeks later. At that session staff facilitators handed out guidelines on giving and receiving feedback. The guidelines were discussed in groups, and then the whole group together formulated rules on how the session should be conducted in a constructive way.

Pairs of students then exchanged assignment plans and discussed them for about 30 minutes. They discussed the legal concepts and rules they needed to answer the question and compared their research findings. The pairs then fed back to the whole group and staff facilitator for another 30 minutes. The groups carried out the exercise around the seventh and eighth weeks of the first semester. The peer-assessment activity boosted their confidence considerably.

Peer feedback

Although not expressly designed for managing assessment in a modular scheme, Maughan and Moore (1999) describe an exercise for law students (see below) that may be used for this purpose. Since first-year students are often ignorant of what their tutors want from them in assignments, planning and writing the first assignment is especially daunting.

Assessment in class

Another in-class technique is described by Elsmore (1999) and reported below. It was aimed at developing in students a strategy for exam preparation without creating unreasonable demands on staffing.

Class tests

At Southampton Institute the core law subjects of contract and tort are assessed by examination only. In the last two sessions before the exam a number of seminars were used to run a closed-book test with up to 15 minutes' response time. It was focused on answer planning and was particularly apt for essay-style exam questions. A summary 'ideal' bullet-style answer would then be distributed and discussed as part of specific revision. It was useful in encouraging solid structure, with theme, opinion and conclusion. Students found the method valuable as they found out how well they could plan with little or no tutor assistance.

This strategy also involved elements of either tutor/student or group marking during the session to enable instant feedback. The marking scheme was available either as a handout or on the OHP and illustrated to the students where marks can be gleaned for detailed analysis, effective application of the facts and solid sourcing and referencing in particular. The session also included some sound practical advice.

Self assessment

Self assessment is used not only to save tutors' time but to develop students' judgement and to help them develop responsibility for their own learning. Self-assessment may take one of several forms, not all of which involve allocating marks (Gibbs, 1995a). According to Hinnett and Thomas (1999), if you are planning to introduce self-assessment you will 'first need to clarify the assessment practices currently used so that [you] understand the scope and nature of changes [you] are proposing'. They provide a useful checklist to help you do this, identifying 14 practices to be aware of. These range from a need for awareness that 'staff carry implicit assessment criteria that they do not articulate to themselves or communicate to other staff and students' to advice that 'students assess their own assignments/projects/exam and negotiate the grade with staff and sometimes peers'.

Self-assessment sheets

Students are given a proforma specific to the type of assignment to be submitted (essays, reviews, lab reports etc.). They complete it and attach it to their assignment. If it is not attached the work is considered incomplete and referred back to the student. Unless students are used to

---

Self and peer assessment on a counselling skills course

Formative, oral self and peer assessment by members of the student group takes place throughout the course during reflection sessions built into the weekly training exercises. Three assignments are self-, peer- and tutor-assessed practical work on a pass/fail basis and students must gain a pass on all the assessment items in order to pass the course. A feedback regime is included in these exercises and students are expected to make notes after each session in order to monitor their progress and accumulate data they can use in their assignments and in the self- and peer-assessment exercises.

Students also undertake a final self and peer assessment (both written and verbal), which is run as a group activity over a period of nine hours and for which they are wholly responsible. Students submit a self assessment of their learning. Each student takes in turn up to ten other students' reports, reads the self assessment and, noting the criteria used and bearing in mind any specific requests for feedback that might have been made, writes a signed peer assessment. Individuals then retrieve their own report and, when they have considered their own and other people's comments, write a second version of their self-report.

The staff believed that the process was working well, primarily because the students took it very seriously, and because they have found that they always agreed with the students' decisions. This success has come about through the care taken in the course design to introduce the idea of self and peer assessment right from the start, and to train and support students in its implementation (Gibbs, 1995c).

using them, self-assessment sheets need to be quite structured and give students ideas about the kinds of things they should be reviewing. This should include criteria and rating scales as well as headings for comments. Self assessment is considered a valuable learning activity in itself; it need not involve students actually awarding themselves marks that count towards the formal assessment system.

Although the use of self assessment may be desirable for pedagogic reasons, it will not necessarily save a module leader time if the marks count towards the formal assessment system. Monitoring is essential and tutors need to retain the right to moderate marks and maintain standards. It is important to recognise what students can and cannot validly judge if their feedback or marks are to be reliable.

Without guidance concerning the criteria you want them to use they may be swayed by surface features and not consider crucial aspects. Criteria need to be explicit, clear, and agreed, which generally requires group discussion.

Summary points

As a module leader wanting to manage marking and maintain feedback it is important that you:

- are aware of the norms for the amount of assessment in a module in your institution and your subject area;

- have identified how to assess the key outcomes for your module;

- put in place assessment methods that will help students learn;

- identify clear criteria by reference to which you can mark or grade work and provide feedback;

- recognise ways in which assessment that helps learning can be carried out in groups or by students themselves;

- provide feedback to students on the learning they are achieving without being yourself overwhelmed by paperwork; and

- maintain proper records so that mistakes are not made in reporting the students' results.

Using evaluation effectively

8

The assessment of quality in teaching is ongoing (and seemingly unending). Those responsible for making judgements are expected to investigate what your subject group does to check the quality of the teaching you provide. Inevitably you will be required to ensure that there is an 'audit trail', i.e. that it is possible to ascertain how you investigated strengths and weaknesses; the conclusions that were drawn about the need for change; and how you changed what you and/or the students did as a consequence. On top of all this, there is the worry that if you find there is a problem with your module, it might count against you if you seek promotion or when your contract comes up for renewal. It is relatively easy in such an atmosphere to lose sight of the fact that if you are a teacher then you want people to learn and you want to change what you do if that will help students learn more or more easily. As Marino (2001) states:

> When you are teaching those who don't want to be in your class, it is hard to get them to evaluate you well. And when you are teaching those that don't belong in your class it is also hard to get them to evaluate you well. But the real art of teaching is to take the disinterested student and help them become interested. The real art of teaching is to take the student that you think can't do it and help them make it through and do so with flying colors. The real art of teaching is to help students learn.

This chapter is brief, suggesting the sorts of issues it is useful to consider when evaluating modules; useful ways of doing quick mid-term evaluations that allow you to make changes for the students being evaluated; and evaluation issues that are important at the course, rather than module level.

Problems associated with evaluating modules

Evaluating modules poses its own challenges. You may not meet the students socially or in other contexts so formal evaluation may be more than usually necessary. Because the student group may be more diverse, so may the views of the students and there may even be distinct subgroups with specific views. Modules often last only one term or semester and you may never see some of the students again. It may be worthwhile to use evaluation early in the module to help the current students rather than later on and only affect next year's module.

Modules may have large enrolments, and so economical and quick methods may be required. Modules have distinctive problems which conventional course evaluation questionnaires may not tap. And, finally, many problems on modules are related to problems on other modules, before or afterwards, and others may need to know your evaluation findings and you theirs.

The following issues are offered as a prompt for the kinds of evaluation questions you might wish to pursue:

- Which modules have students taken before they tackle this module? Are there distinct sub-groups with clearly identifiable module profiles?

- Do students arrive with appropriate background knowledge?

- Do different student sub-groups have different background knowledge?

- Is there overlap between the content or process of your module and some of the modules your students take elsewhere?

- Does the module start at the right level for (all) students?

- Does the module progress at the right pace for (all) students?

- Does the module cover an appropriate amount of material for (all) students?

- Do (all) students understand the academic conventions involved in your module (or discipline)?

- Do (all) students have the appropriate study skills for your module (or discipline)?

- Do all groups of students succeed equally well?

- Do the module's tasks and assignments generate an appropriate workload (as planned and described in the module documentation)?

- Does the module produce an acceptable average mark and distribution of marks in relation to other modules?

- Which parts, skills or concepts do (different) students have most difficulty with?

- Does the module prepare students appropriately for the modules they go on to?

- What do lecturers from other subject areas, from which some of the students are drawn, think of your module and what it achieves?

Check your hunches

Many modular courses have adopted standardised student feedback questionnaires so as to allow managers to make comparisons across modules. A subject group may require all modules to be evaluated each time they run, but leave the form of the evaluation entirely up to module leaders so that topical and relevant issues can be explored properly. More commonly now formal evaluation follows a cycle so that each module is evaluated once in, say, three years. The institution may have a particular agenda to address in a given year which will give a particular slant to the evaluation that you are *required* to do.

These evaluations may not help module leaders improve the teaching and learning on their own module(s) since standard questionnaires seldom address the issues which are important to the module leader. It is important then that, even where standard questionnaires are used, you follow up your own hunches about what is going on in your module with your own idiosyncratic evaluation. If you are using a questionnaire then these hunches can simply be shared with students to see if they believe the same as you do about what is going on. The sorts of questions you might ask are shown in Figure 8.1

Fig. 8.1: Testing your hunches

	Strongly agree	Agree	Unsure	Disagree	Strongly disagree
1 If you hadn't already done Module 4520 then this module was too hard.					
2 The workload was too heavy compared with other modules.					
3 The mix of students was more of a help than a hindrance.					

Don't leave it until the end

Modularisation has increased the volume of evaluation by increasing the number of course units to be evaluated and reducing the ease with which informal evaluation can be undertaken. Students are often on other modules before the evaluation results are even collated and they may never encounter the same tutor again so they seldom experience any direct benefit from evaluation. As a result they quickly exhibit 'evaluation fatigue' and stop returning questionnaires or taking them seriously. If you want students to help you to improve your module you may need to seek their feedback early enough to allow you to act on some of the implications immediately so that you may benefit them there and then. Even for those issues which you cannot act on until next time the module runs, you need to let the students see what you intend to do before they lose interest in the module.

The next section of this chapter suggests some simple ways to get feedback on your module. Hounsell, Tait and Day's (1997) *Feedback on Courses and Programmes of Study*, Harvey's (1998) *Evaluation Cookbook*, and Gibbs, Habeshaw and Habeshaw's (1988) *53 Interesting Ways to Improve Your Teaching* all have many more suggestions for evaluation of modules and courses.

Get instant feedback

Getting feedback quickly from students during a module can be difficult using conventional methods, especially if your module is large and you do not see your students much. You will need quick and convenient methods, probably administered during class time. Here are some suggestions:

- sample rather than ask everyone – this can involve only administering questionnaires to rows three and five in the lecture hall (never ask the back row!) or only asking one or two of the seminar groups; and

- ask for a show of hands in class in response to simple questions – for example, 'Who would like me, next week, to go back over the material we've dealt with so far in the course and to drop one of the topics we have left?' 'If I offered a remedial problem class on X for students who haven't encountered this before, who would come along?' 'Who would like me to go faster/at a higher level/slower/at a more basic level?'

Instant questionnaires

This involves writing on the board or overhead projector three to five statements about the course (such as those suggested in 'Check your hunches') and asking students to indicate if they agree with them or not. Students may use a piece of their own paper and give their responses on a five point scale (1 = strongly agree, 2 = agree, 3 = unsure, 4 = disagree, 5 = strongly disagree); they need only number and not write down the statements. They then hand these pieces of paper in as they leave the class. Their 'instant questionnaires' should be anonymous and look like Figure 8.2.

Fig. 8.2: Results from an instant questionnaire

Q	A
1.	1
2.	3
3.	2
4.	5
5.	1

With instant questionnaires, there is no need to plan in advance, type up and print questionnaires or spend time circulating pieces of paper. You can quickly collate the data from these sheets and report back to students the following week:

1 Last week in the instant questionnaire you told me that it was not the case that 'if you hadn't already done Module 4520 then this module was too hard'.

2 However you did think the workload was heavy compared with other modules. I've responded by cutting back on the amount of data involved in the exercises for the remaining practical sessions.

3 You disagreed with each other about whether the mix of students was more of a help than a hindrance. I'm not sure what to make of that. If anyone has any good ideas could you take me for a coffee after this session and explain them?

You must always treat such surveys with caution. One extensive course-wide evaluation at Oxford Brookes University showed that every module students took had a heavier workload than the others! To avoid such problems it may be important to make questions more specific, for example, 'It took more than 3 hours to work out the answers to problem sheet 2'.

Coffee groups

Informal chatting with a small group of students is very useful when you are unsure what questions to ask or hunches to pursue in questionnaires. A quick and congenial way to undertake informal evaluation is to convene a 'coffee group' – six or so students drawn from across the module whom you meet with over a coffee and cakes (at your department's expense!) once a fortnight. Their role is simply to keep you in touch with how things are going – what is working and what is not – and especially about those aspects of the module not visible to lecturers such as what students do with their time and whether library books are accessible. They should be requested to ask around their friends for their views though there are limits to how representative such a group can be. Where there are many parallel seminar or laboratory groups it can be useful to form a feedback group by selecting one member from each seminar or lab. If there are distinct subgroups, such as students from three other subject areas outside your own, then these should be represented. Issues that emerge about which you are sceptical can be quickly checked out quantitatively (see 'Get instant feedback' above) or you can request the group to ask around specifically about that issue and report back at the next coffee meeting.

Tracking student groups

It is common for student performance on a module, and their views about the module, to be strongly linked to their past experience and performance on preceding modules. For example, students who have taken and done well on a particular first-year science module may succeed on and like a challenging second-year module. Those who either did not take or did badly on the first-year module may fail or hate the second-year module. Improvements may be more appropriate in the first-year module. Students leaving your module may also use what they have learnt in a limited number of alternative modules afterwards. How well they do on these modules and how well you have prepared them may be more important than whether or not they like your module or think you are a good teacher. A vital part of the evaluation of modules is tracking student groups to see which perform well and respond well and which do not, and why. Strictly speaking this should be the responsibility of the subject group and one of the things that it requires a module leader to do. It can be nearly impossible for a module leader to do this if colleagues teaching related modules are unwilling to cooperate.

Module report forms

It is easy for modules to be evaluated as if they were entirely freestanding and unconnected with anything else. Communication of evaluation findings to the course leader and to others teaching related modules is crucial. The module report form shown in Figure 8.3 provides a basic proforma for this purpose.

Such a report form, used for all modules in a subject area, would identify common issues and proposals for change that could be acted on cooperatively across modules.

Fig. 8.3: Module report form

Module title	3501 Introduction to Egyptology
Tutor(s)	T. Khamen
Semester/year	Semester 2, 2002/3
No of students	125
Evaluation agenda	Background knowledge of students without A-level Egyptology Adequacy of library stocks Development of skills in Egyptology for application in module 3502: Pyramid technology
Evaluation evidence collected	Standard questionnaire Pretest results Discussion session with students on 3502
Issues to be addressed by subject area	A-level scores do not relate to performance on 3501 and should not be used for selection A standard approach to format and marking criteria for fieldwork reports is required Fund development and copyright clearance of reading resources to supplement library stocks
Proposed changes for next operation of module	Pretest to be retained and backed up by additional practical sessions in weeks 2–4 for those that need them Training in report writing to be introduced Criteria used for assessment of reports to be published
Evaluation agenda for next operation of module	More detailed evaluation of students in 3502 to test adequacy of preparation by 3501

It has the following features:

- it is short and should be quick and easy to complete;

- it should be easy to review a collection of such reports quickly in order to see how a subject area or a pathway within a subject area is getting on;

- it allows the subject area or course leader to set an evaluation agenda based on last year's evaluation or current concerns;

- it requires evidence to be collected so that the basis of the report is clear and fact may be distinguished from opinion;

- it does not require the evidence itself to be reported, so retaining confidentiality and saving paper;

- it identifies issues that require the attention of colleagues and action the module leader cannot undertake alone or without resources;

- it identifies changes which are planned in the light of evaluation, so that colleagues who teach related modules can see the implications for them; and

- it identifies an evaluation agenda for the following year.

Summary points

As a module leader wanting to evaluate effectively, it is important that you:

- are aware of evaluation agendas set by your institution and standard methods of evaluation you are expected to use;

- are aware of any issues that are important to your subject group or department and how they impact on your module;

- are aware of any wider issues of quality associated with evaluation of your module;

- find out how students are responding to the various learning activities you organise; and

- devise ways of getting some feedback on key aspects of the module and that you show students how you respond to it.

Appendix 1

Descriptor for a qualification at honours (H) level – bachelor's degree with honours

Honours degrees are awarded to students who have demonstrated:

i   a systematic understanding of key aspects of their field of study, including acquisition of coherent and detailed knowledge, at least some of which is at or informed by, the forefront of defined aspects of a discipline;

ii   an ability to deploy accurately established techniques of analysis and enquiry within a discipline;

iii   conceptual understanding that enables the student:
- to devise and sustain arguments, and/or to solve problems, using ideas and techniques, some of which are at the forefront of a discipline; and
- to describe and comment upon particular aspects of current research, or equivalent advanced scholarship, in the discipline;

iv   an appreciation of the uncertainty, ambiguity and limits of knowledge; and

v   the ability to manage their own learning, and to make use of scholarly reviews and primary sources (e.g. refereed research articles and/or original materials appropriate to the discipline).

Typically, holders of the qualification will be able to:

a   apply the methods and techniques that they have learned to review, consolidate, extend and apply their knowledge and understanding, and to initiate and carry out projects;

b   critically evaluate arguments, assumptions, abstract concepts and data (that may be incomplete), to make judgements, and to frame appropriate questions to achieve a solution – or identify a range of solutions – to a problem; and

c   communicate information, ideas, problems, and solutions to both specialist and non-specialist audiences;

and will have:

d   qualities and transferable skills necessary for employment requiring:
- the exercise of initiative and personal responsibility;
- decision-making in complex and unpredictable contexts; and
- the learning ability needed to undertake appropriate further training of a professional or equivalent nature.

Source: QAA (2001a) p. 12

Appendix 2

Contents of typical QAA subject standards consultation documents

The consultation documents though similar in different subjects are by no means the same in the way the information is presented, as the comparison in the table below shows.

Contents of typical QAA subject standards consultation documents

Academic standards – psychology	Academic standards - physics, astronomy and astrophysics
1 Introduction	1 Introduction
2 Defining principles	2 Nature and extent of the subject
3 Nature and extent of the discipline	3 Subject knowledge and understanding

4 Knowledge and skills
4a Subject knowledge
  4a i Preamble
  4a ii Knowledge domains
  4a iii Examples of topic areas within core domains
4b Skills
  4b i Preamble
  4b ii Subject skills......
  4b iii Generic skills.....
	4 Subject-based skills and other skills
	  4.1 Physics skills
	  4.2 Transferable skills

5 Teaching, learning and assessment 5a Preamble 5b Teaching and learning 5c Assessment	5 Teaching, learning and assessment

6 Benchmark statements
6a Preamble
6b Subject knowledge statements
  6b i Threshold
  6b ii Modal
6c Subject skills statements
  6c i Threshold
  6c ii Modal
6d Generic skills statements
  6d i Threshold
  6d ii Modal
	6 Academic standards of attainment
	Bachelors degree
	Threshold attainment
	Bachelors degree
	Typical attainment

Example 1 – detailed specification of knowledge in psychology

Extracted from QAA Academic Standards, Draft for Consultation, July 2001 (QAA, 2001b)

4a ii   Knowledge domains

It is not the intention to be overly prescriptive in defining the subject knowledge acquired by students; nevertheless, there are certain core areas within the discipline which should each receive significant coverage. Students should also be exposed to novel developments in the discipline, including those that at present do not command consensus.

4a iii   Examples of topic areas within core domains

The examples in the topics which follow are given to indicate the scope of each of the areas. They are intended to be neither prescriptive nor exhaustive, and it is recognised that the topics covered will vary from institution to institution and over time. Knowledge of both of the areas and of the links between them is expected, as is an understanding of appropriate applications. Ethical, theoretical and practical research issues are common to each of the knowledge areas within psychology:

- biological psychology;
- cognitive psychology;
- developmental psychology;
- personality and individual differences; and
- social psychology (examples omitted in each case).

It is expected that all the main sub-areas listed below will be covered

Research methods in psychology, i.e. research design, the nature and appropriate statistical analysis of data, psychometrics and measurement techniques, and quantitative and qualitative methods.

It should be noted that qualitative methods are understood broadly here, and might include protocol analysis, interviews, grounded theory and discourse analysis.

Example 2 – detailed specification of skills in physics

Extract from QAA Academic Standards, Draft for Consultation, July 2001 (QAA, 2001c)

4   Subject-based skills and other skills

Honours and masters degrees in physics will develop a wide range of competence in transferable and subject-specific skills of which the following are particularly relevant:

4.1   Physics skills

Students should learn:

- how to formulate and tackle problems in physics. For example, ... how to present the solution making their assumptions and approximations explicit;

- how to plan, execute and report the results of an experiment or investigation. .... They should also be able to relate any conclusions they make to current theories of the physics involved; and

- how to use mathematics to describe the physical world.

4.2   Transferable skills

A physics degree should enhance:

- **Problem-solving skills**
  Physics degree programmes involve students in solving problems with well-defined solutions. ... They should develop the confidence to try different approaches in order to make progress on challenging problems.

- **Investigative skills**
  Students will have opportunities to develop their skills of independent investigation. ...

- **Communication skills**
  Physics and the mathematics used in physics deal with surprising ideas and difficult concepts; good communication is essential. A physics degree should develop students' ability to listen carefully, to read demanding texts, and to present complex information in a clear and concise manner.

- **Analytical skills**
  Physics helps students learn the need to pay attention to detail and to develop their ability to manipulate precise and intricate ideas, to construct logical arguments and to use technical language correctly.

- **IT skills**
  During their studies, students will develop their computing and IT skills in a variety of ways, including their ability to use appropriate software such as programming languages and packages.

- **Personal skills**
  Students should develop their ability to work independently, to use their initiative, to organise themselves to meet deadlines, and to interact constructively with other people.

Example 3 – detailed specification of teaching, learning and assessment in music

Extract from QAA Academic Standards, Draft for Consultation, July 2001 (QAA, 2001d)

(Author's note: This example from music, specifies a large variety of small group work in its teaching and learning methods. In contrast only 'lectures supported by problem classes and group tutorial work; laboratory work' are specified for physics.)

5   Teaching, learning and assessment

5.1   Programme design

5.1.1   As noted elsewhere, the study of music at HE level is intrinsically multi-disciplinary and cross-cultural, covering a wide range of skills and intellectual abilities. …

5.1.2   The multiplicity of music curricula across the HE sector is a strength …

5.1.3   Music provision in HE covers a broad spectrum from composition and performance-based programmes to those more focused on text-based studies or technology, … it is generally assumed that aural-analytical skills, and the knowledge of one or more repertoires and their associated techniques and traditions of performance and reception, are fundamental to the study of the discipline.

5.2   Progression

5.3   Teaching and learning methods

5.3.1   The teaching of music, especially in the areas of creative practice, normally involves a substantial component of individual or small-group teaching. Much of the best teaching is an interactive process … The interaction between teaching, research (which includes the informed expertise of creative practitioners in performance and composition) and scholarship is a key element in the study of music … (and) underpins the most stimulating teaching and learning environments.

5.3.2   Quality assurance methodology requires documentation outlining aims and objectives for programmes and their constituent elements, and explaining how assessment methods are appropriate to designated learning outcomes. … typically an honours music undergraduate would experience at some stage most of the following:

- **lectures** that stimulate thought, discussion and debate, and which encourage further reading, listening and research by which students can extend their own knowledge and understanding;

- **seminars** or other forms of small group discussion, sometimes … to develop oral presentation, negotiation and communication skills;

- other forms of **small-group** teaching and learning in which students have the opportunity to work together as a team;

- **one-to-one** interaction, particularly supporting the development of self-direction, intellectual independence and research skills through dissertations, analysis and individual projects, and the development of creative skills through composition and performance;

- **individual or small group** vocal or instrumental instruction … ;

- **corporate performance activity**, groups ranging in size from small ensembles to large choirs and orchestras, developing teamwork and leadership skills;

- **workshops and masterclasses**, normally addressing the acquisition of creative skills and techniques within a group context … ;

- **essay-writing** as a means of developing research techniques, acquiring knowledge, and presenting ideas and arguments in written form;

- **practical exercises** … ;

- **use of C&IT**, including computer-assisted learning … ;

- **studio or laboratory work**, including hands-on experience in the use of electronic equipment;

- **independent learning** … ;

- **external placements**, often with a vocational slant … ;

- **fieldwork projects**, where students study a musical culture in situ …;

- a wide variety of **extra-curricular activities** … ;

- **peer learning**, where students discuss critically their colleagues' work … .

(Author's note: much detail has been left out for the sake of brevity but hopefully without distorting the sense.)

Appendix 3

Examples of subject pathways and programme outcomes

3

The first example is for a major subject pathway in a modular scheme. Although this terminology is common, it does not have a unique definition and does not imply a specific proportion of subject-based study in different schemes. The term 'pathway' also implies that the scheme is constructed from an array of modules from which a meaningful programme may be followed, whereas the terms 'subject' or 'field' imply that the modules are first constructed to create a programme and then set in an array. Since there is no defined general usage the terms may be used differently in some institutions. The extracts provided below are limited for space reasons and are used to illustrate the specification of:

- main educational aims of the scheme or field (section 9);

- programme outcomes of:
  - knowledge and understanding, teaching and learning srategies and methods;
  - cognitive (thinking) skills, teaching and learning strategies and methods (section 10);
- requirements for route / pathway / field, levels, modules, credits and awards (section 11).

Sections 1–8 of the specifications are basic facts about the institution, the name of the award, etc.

Programme specification for a major subject pathway in a modular scheme

Extract from QAA Guidelines (2002) Example 4A

Outcomes statements have been referenced to the geography benchmarking statement (G) and the institution's policy for skill development in the undergraduate modular scheme (I).

9   Main educational aims of the scheme or field

The two principal substantive themes in the human geography field are the geography of economic change and the interpretation of social and cultural landscapes. There is a subsidiary theme in development studies. The main aims are:

- to develop the intellectual and practical skills of the student in the collection, analysis, interpretation and understanding of geographic data and information with specific reference to social, cultural and economic aspects of the geographic environment (G);

- to prepare students for employment in a wide range of contexts or for further study and a career where human geographic knowledge and skills will be applied (I);

- to enable students to engage with life-long learning, study and enquiry, and to appreciate the value of education to society (G & I).

10 Programme outcomes – the route/pathway/field provides opportunities for students to achieve and demonstrate the following learning outcomes

Knowledge and understanding	Teaching and learning strategies and methods
1 sense of place, place identity, landscape construction (G) 2 time–space relationship, globalisation and global interconnections (G) 3 the various processes actively changing the economic, social and cultural landscape (G) 4 local distinctiveness, difference and similarity of place, and interdependence (G) 5 development theory and 'Third World' identity (G) 6 principles, theory, philosophy and practice of human geography (G)	**Core knowledge and understanding** (1–5) is acquired via lectures, practicals, seminars, fieldwork, and guided independent study, while more 'advanced' knowledge and understanding (6) is obtained by the former as well as through independent study and specific group team work. **Assessment – knowledge and understanding** (1–6) is assessed via examination (seen and unseen) and coursework.
Cognitive (thinking) skills – able to:	
7 assemble data from a variety of sources and discern and establish connections (G & I) 8 synthesise and evaluate primary and secondary data (G & I) 9 critically analyse literature on human geography (G) 10 apply human geographic principles, theories and methods to the investigation of field themes (G) 11 plan, conduct and report an individual research programme (G & I)	**Cognitive skills** (7–11) are promoted via lectures, practicals, seminars and group discussions, tutorials and group work. Learning to apply these thinking skills to human geography issues is obtained via case studies and in particular fieldwork. **Assessment – cognitive skills** (7–11) are assessed by coursework and examinations. Examinations provide students with the opportunity to demonstrate their ability to structure a clear, concise, reasoned argument and analyse an issue in a limited time period. The execution of a dissertation and an optional independent study at level 3 allows a student to demonstrate his/her thinking skills to the highest level.

11 Route/pathway/field requirements, levels, modules, credits and awards

The programme is offered in full-time and part-time mode.

Human geography is concerned with interpreting the creation and transformation of space, place and landscape from a wide range of economic, social, political and cultural processes. It is concerned to analyse these processes at different scales – local, national, international and global – and over varying time periods.

Students study two fields in either major:minor or joint combination (major: minor = 15+5 modules, joint=10 modules in both fields). The modular programme allows students to structure their programme of study within certain prescribed limits. Major and joint students in human geography should satisfy scheme and field requirements at each level to allow them to graduate with their designated degree title, see details below. Compulsory modules at levels 1 and 2 are prerequisites for certain level 2 and 3 modules (see below). Optional modules give students the opportunity to construct individualised 'pathways' of their choice within the field. All fields are underpinned by a common compulsory 'skills' programme (2 modules) at level 1.

Prerequisites operate for the following modules:

Level 2 modules	**Level 1 prerequisites**
Fieldweek	Making Places and Global Development Issues
Investigating Society	Making Places and Global Development Issues
Landscapes in Transition	Making Places
Geography of Economic Change	Global Development Issues

Level 3 modules	**Level 2 prerequisites**
Dissertation	Fieldweek and Investigating Society
Interdisciplinary Study	Fieldweek and Investigating Society
Society, Space and Social Science	Investigating Society
Independent Study	Investigating Society

Award requirements:

For the honours degree human geography (major) students should:

- pass 26 module credits (10 at level 1 and 8 at level 2 and 8 at level 3);

- achieve a minimum of 15 module credits in a major field and a minimum of 5 credits in a minor field;

- pass both the level 1 undergraduate scheme skills modules;

- satisfy the field progression requirements at level 1 and 2;

- complete the two credits of dissertation and the level 3 compulsory module;

- achieve a total of 360 credits.

The second example is for one half of a joint honours degree and illustrates the specification of:

- programme aims;
- programme outcomes:
  - knowledge and understanding, teaching, learning and assessment methods;
  - key skills, teaching, learning and assessment methods;
- programme structure.

Programme specification for one half of a joint programme

Extract from QAA Guidelines (2001) Example 5

9 Programme aims

- to provide students with at least a basic knowledge and understanding of selected foundation subjects of English law to enable them to satisfy the requirements set by the Law Society and the Bar Council for the academic stage of legal training with only one further year of legal study;
- to enable students to extend their legal knowledge and understanding beyond the selected foundation subjects by providing other selected law modules in areas which are intellectually or professionally complementary to their scientific studies and which provide some insight into the scientific contextualisation of the law;
- to provide a specific grounding in cognate scientific and legal subjects so as to enable students to appreciate and understand the interface between two technical disciplines and their use in modern industrial society;
- to enable students to identify, locate and critically appraise legal materials;
- to enable students to assimilate extensive documentary legal and some non-legal materials and to extract from them the material points;
- to apply the principles of law and legal rules to solve and analyse practical problems, and to reason logically, supporting the process with authority;
- to provide students with the necessary intellectual and practical legal skills, such as analysis, problem-solving and legal reasoning, to enable them independently to achieve a basic understanding of any branch of English law even if they had not previously studied it;
- to provide students with the necessary personal and key skills to enable them to develop as independent, autonomous and reflective individuals;
- to provide students with the opportunity to enhance and develop their written and oral communication skills; and
- to prepare students for graduate employment by developing their transferable and problem-based learning skills.

10 Programme outcomes

Programme outcomes that relate directly to the threshold outcomes in the law subject benchmarking statement are indicated by L.

Students who gain the award will have demonstrated knowledge and understanding, skills, qualities and other attributes in the following areas:

- **Knowledge and understanding – a student will be expected to**:
  - demonstrate at least a basic knowledge of the theory, principles, conceptual framework and methodology of the selected law modules of stud;.
  - L demonstrate that the law modules of his or her programme have been studied in depth;
  - be aware of and understand current developments in English law in the subjects of study;
  - demonstrate the basic principles and techniques of legal research in English law; and
  - have an understanding of some of the relevant social, economic, political, historical, philosophical, ethical, scientific and cultural contexts within which the law operates.

- **Teaching, learning and assessment methods used to enable outcomes to be achieved and demonstrated:** lectures; tutor-led workshops; tutor-led seminars; prepared problem-based lectures; essays.

- **Assessment**: seen or unseen written examinations; open-book examinations; assessed essays; dissertation.

- **Subject-specific skills and other attributes**

S **Key skills – a student will be expected to:**
  - L communicate effectively to others when working in a group;
  - L evaluate and assess his or her own abilities, performance and understanding, to reflect on his or her own learning and to seek advice and feedback;
  - give at least a basic oral presentation using some presentation tools;
  - L use some electronic information management tools, which will probably include word-processing, email, use of the world wide web and some electronic information retrieval systems;
  - utilise problem-solving skills in theoretical or practical contexts;
  - take responsibility for his/her own learning and personal and professional development.;
  - manage time and prioritise tasks by working to strict deadlines; and
  - be aware of key career opportunities and the need for forward planning – this is a desirable learning outcome but it is not assessed and students need not demonstrate this in order to obtain even an honours degree.

- **Teaching, learning and assessment methods used to enable outcomes to be achieved and demonstrated:** transferable skills permeate every activity within the programme content and assessment – examinations, presentations, workshops, PESCA (a computer-based skills profiling tool used by individuals to identify their own learning and to plan for their own development).

11 Programme structures and requirements, levels, modules, credits and awards

The programme is studied over three years and is university-based throughout that time. Study is undertaken at three levels, one for each year of study. The programme is divided into units of study called modules. Modules have a credit rating of either 15 or 30 credits, but most are 30 credits and take place over all three terms. Each level comprises 120 credits.

- The innovative feature of this programme is the combination of two discrete disciplines through the study of cognate subjects.

- A distinctive feature of the law component of the programme is the three-tier approach of interactive lectures, student consultations and workshops that emphasise both legal knowledge and understanding as well as the acquisition of legal and interpersonal skills.

- The law modules have been carefully selected to complement the study of a science.

- Students who obtain the degree at least with a second-class honours may apply to take the BA (law) degree in their fourth year. If the appropriate modules are chosen, this provides the same exemptions from the first stage of the law professional examinations as the LL.B degree.

	Units of study	Credit	Potential awards
HE Level 1	**second subject module**	(30)	
	second subject module	(30)	
	Law of Contract	30	
	Public Law of UK and EU 1	30	
HE Level 2	**second subject module**	(30)	
	second subject module	(30)	
	Law of Torts	30	
	Employment Law	30	
HE Level 3	**second subject module**	(30)	
	second subject module	(30)	
	Intellectual Property	30	
	Company Law	30	
		360	BSc (Hons)

Appendix 4

SEEC Generic levels descriptors

4

These descriptors differ from the original SEEC/HECIW descriptors mainly in the layout, in the inclusion of references to key skills and in the inclusion of the two levels for postgraduate study (currently under consultation at time of writing).

The level descriptors: some important notes

- Areas of learning differ according to the extent to which the knowledge or skills developed are **generic** or more **subject specific**. The areas of learning are labelled accordingly.

- In general, progression is characterised by two important related factors:

  i   the **autonomy** of the learner; and

  ii the increasing **responsibility** that is expected of the learner in the guidance given and the task set.

- Under the heading Practical skills (subject specific) some or all of the following skills will be identified by subject specialists at any level; it will be useful for subject specialists to develop more detailed descriptors of these skills, where relevant, to determine achievement at each level:

  a   investigative skills/methods of enquiry;

  b   laboratory skills/fieldcraft;

  c   data and information processing/IT;

  d   content/textual analysis;

  e   performance skills;

  f   product development;

  g   professional skills;

  h   spatial awareness; and

  i   management of resources.

- The version of the level descriptors given here has been adapted slightly from the official version approved by the SEEC General Council to enable the level descriptors to be more easily used for staff development purposes.

HE Level 1 (NQF:C)

Development of knowledge and understanding (subject specific)

The learner:

- **Knowledge base:** has a given factual and/or conceptual knowledge base with emphasis on the nature of the field of study and appropriate terminology;
- **Ethical issues:** can demonstrate awareness of ethical issues in current areas of study and is able to discuss these in relation to personal beliefs and values.

Cognitive/intellectual skills (generic)

The learner:

- **Analysis:** can analyse with guidance using given classifications/principles;
- **Synthesis:** can collect and categorise ideas and information in a predictable and standard format;
- **Evaluation:** can evaluate the reliability of data using defined techniques and/or tutor guidance;
- **Application:** can apply given tools/methods accurately and carefully to a well defined problem and begin to appreciate the complexity of the issues.

Key/transferable skills (generic)

The learner:

- **Group working:** can work effectively with others as a member of a group and meet obligations to others (for example, tutors, peers and colleagues);
- **Learning resources:** can work within an appropriate ethos and can use and access a range of learning resources;
- **Self evaluation:** can evaluate own strengths and weaknesses within criteria largely set by others;
- **Management of information:** can manage information, collect appropriate data from a range of sources and undertake simple research tasks with external guidance;
- **Autonomy:** can take responsibility for own learning with appropriate support;
- **Communications:** can communicate effectively in a format appropriate to the discipline(s) and report practical procedures in a clear and concise manner;
- **Problem solving:** can apply given tools/methods accurately to a well defined problem and begins to appreciate the complexity of the issues in the discipline.

Practical skills (subject specific)

The learner:

- **Application of skills:** can operate in predictable, defined contexts that require use of a specified range of standard techniques;
- **Autonomy in skill use:** is able to act with limited autonomy, under direction or supervision, within defined guidelines;

HE Level 2 (NQF:I)

Development of knowledge and understanding (subject specific)

The learner:
- Knowledge base: has a detailed knowledge of major theories of the discipline(s) and an awareness of a variety of ideas, contexts and frameworks;
- Ethical issues: is aware of the wider social and environmental implications of area(s) of study and is able to debate issues in relation to more general ethical perspectives.

Cognitive/intellectual skills (generic)

The learner:
- Analysis: can analyse a range of information with minimum guidance using given classifications/principles and can compare alternative methods and techniques for obtaining data;
- Synthesis: can format a range of ideas and information towards a given purpose;
- Evaluation: can select appropriate techniques of evaluation and can evaluate the relevance and significance of the data collected;
- Application: can identify key elements of problems and choose appropriate methods for their resolution in a considered manner.

Key/transferable skills (generic)

The learner:
- Group working: can interact effectively within a team/learning group, giving and receiving information and ideas and modifying responses where appropriate;
- Learning resources: can manage learning using resources for the discipline; can develop working relationships of a professional nature within the discipline(s);
- Self evaluation: can evaluate own strengths and weaknesses, challenge received opinion and develop own criteria and judgement;
- Management of information: can manage information; can select appropriate data from a range of sources and develop appropriate research strategies;
- Autonomy: can take responsibility for own learning with minimum direction;
- Communications: can communicate effectively in a manner appropriate to the discipline(s) and report practical procedures in a clear and concise manner in a variety of formats;
- Problem solving: can identify key areas of problems and choose appropriate tools/methods for their resolution in a considered manner.

Practical skills (subject specific)

The learner:
- Application of skills: can operate in situations of varying complexity and predictability requiring application of a wide range of techniques;
- Autonomy in skill use: able to act with increasing autonomy, with reduced need for supervision and direction, within defined guidelines.

Reproduced with permission from Southern England Consortium for Credit Accumulation and Transfer (SEEC) (2001), How to Use Learning Outcomes and Assessment Criteria, *pp. 43–45*

5 Appendix 5

Standards of assessment

Comparison of specification of standards for psychology and physics

Standards of assessment are clearly important and a comparison of the statements about them which appear in the consultative documents for psychology (QAA, 2001b) and physics (QAA, 2001a) are shown in the table below. In the section from the physics consultative paper, there is a statement, which seems to imply that all the threshold statements must be applicable to any student who is given the award. In fact the Code of Practice makes explicit reference to the need to be cautious about 'whether compensation for, and condonation of, failure, should be allowed, particularly within credit-based systems' (QAA, 2000, p. 11) but it is not clear how this is appropriately applied to the assessment of outcomes in individual modules.

Comparison of specification of standards for psychology and physics

Psychology	Physics
6 Benchmark statements	**6 Academic standards of attainment**
6a Preamble The following benchmark statements are divided into two categories:	6.1 All students graduating with honours degrees in physics are expected to demonstrate that they have acquired knowledge, abilities and skills in the areas identified in the previous sections, but there will inevitably exist significant differences in their level of attainment. In particular, there will be differences between the level of attainment demonstrated by a typical student graduating from the bachelors course and a typical student graduating from the masters course.
Threshold standards are the minimal standards necessary for a student to graduate with a single honours degree in psychology.	
Modal standards are those which a typical psychology student would be expected to attain in order to graduate.	6.2 In discussing the range of knowledge and levels of attainment in this section the topics to be covered are those outlined in section 3.
The statements are phrased in terms of what knowledge or skills a graduate at that level (threshold or modal) would be expected to be able to demonstrate.	6.3 It is the learning outcomes, contained within a programme specification, that are assessed and it is the responsibility of institutions to ensure that their regulations and procedures guarantee the integrity of their awards. Compensation is the responsibility of institutions and is therefore not addressed in the benchmark statement. Where an institution allows compensation or condonement it should ensure that that the procedures guarantee that the threshold standards are met. The elements of the threshold criteria appropriate to a joint or dual honours programme are a matter for the institution to determine, possibly through the programme specification.
These threshold statements apply to students in single honours psychology. Students on combined or joint honours programmes will be expected to achieve an appropriate subset of these standards and of those for their other discipline(s).	

Comparison of threshold and modal statements for standards in psychology

In **psychology** the close parallel between the **threshold** and **modal** statements is illustrated below; the latter being an extension or qualification of the former. (Differences are **highlighted** and additions *italicised*.)

Comparison of threshold and modal statements for standards in psychology

6b Subject knowledge statements	
6b i Threshold:	**6b ii Modal:**
• understands the scientific underpinnings of psychology as a discipline;	• *... its historical origins, development; and limitations;*
• recognises the inherent variability and diversity of psychological functioning;	• *... and its significance.*
• can demonstrate a good knowledge and critical understanding of a range of influences on psychological functioning and how they are conceptualised across the core areas as outlined in Section 4a iii;	• *... and how they interrelate.*
• is **knowledgeable** about **a number** of specialised areas and / or applications;	• has **detailed knowledge** of **several** specialised areas and / or applications, *some of which are at the cutting edge of research in the discipline;*
• can demonstrate knowledge of a range of research paradigms, research methods and measurement techniques, including statistical analysis.	• can demonstrate a **systematic** knowledge of a range ... and measurement techniques, including statistical analysis, *and be aware of their limitations.*

Comparison of benchmarks for threshold performance in psychology and physics

The next table shows the benchmarks for threshold performance in psychology and physics. It illustrates the different approaches in the two subjects. 'Demonstration of ability' which is used in physics is replaced by 'can' in psychology. In neither case is there any attempt to lay down rules for interpreting the terms .

Comparison of benchmarks for threshold performance

Psychology	Physics
6b Subject knowledge statements **6b i Threshold:** • understands the scientific underpinnings of psychology as a discipline; • recognises the inherent variability and diversity of psychological functioning; • can demonstrate a good knowledge and critical understanding of a range of influences on psychological functioning and how they are conceptualised across the core areas as outlined in Section 4a iii; • is knowledgeable about a number of specialised areas and/or applications; • can demonstrate knowledge of a range of research paradigms, research methods and measurement techniques, including statistical analysis. **6c Subject skills statements** **6c i Threshold:** • can reason scientifically and demonstrate the relationship between theory and evidence; • can adopt multiple perspectives; • can detect meaningful patterns in behaviour and experience; • can pose and operationalise research questions; • can demonstrate competence in research skills through practical activities; • can reason statistically and demonstrate competence in a range of statistical methods; • can initiate, design, conduct and report an empirically-based research project under appropriate supervision; • is aware of ethical principles and can demonstrate this in relation to personal study, particularly with regard to the research project. **6d Generic skills statements** **6d i Threshold:** • can communicate ideas and research findings by written, oral and visual means; • can interpret and use numerical, statistical and other forms of data; • is computer literate, at least in the use of word processing, databases and statistical software; • can approach problem solving in a systematic way; • is aware of contextual and interpersonal factors in groups and teams; • can undertake self-directed study and project management in a supportive environment; • recognises the need to assess their own skills and to harness them for future learning.	**Bachelors degree** **Threshold attainment:** *Honours degrees should be awarded to students who have demonstrated:* • a basic knowledge and understanding of physical laws and principles, and some application of these principles; • an ability to identify relevant principles and laws when dealing with problems; • the ability to execute and analyse the results of an experiment or investigation; students should be able to evaluate the level of uncertainty in their results and compare these results with expected outcomes, theoretical predictions or published data and hence assess their significance; • competent use of appropriate IT packages/systems for the analysis of data and the retrieval of appropriate information; • an ability in numerical manipulation and the ability to present and interpret information graphically; • an ability to communicate scientific information, in particular through scientific reports; • an ability to manage their own learning and to make use of appropriate texts and learning materials; • a familiarity with basic laboratory apparatus if on an experimental programme.

Bibliography

AAHESGIT (60), Pros and cons of online learning, *Washington Computer User*, October 2000, p. 21, quoted in AAHESGIT-60, 1/11/00

AAHESGIT has recently changed its name to TLT-SWG. Anyone can subscribe to the TLT-SWG Listserver for free by sending the email message (with subject line left blank):
SUBSCRIBE TLT-SWG yourfirstname yourlastname
to LISTPROC@LIST.CREN.NET. For general information about TLT-SWG (or AAHESGIT), see the Listserv/TLT-SWG section of WWW.TLTGROUP.ORG .
For access to TLT-SWG and AAHESGIT Archives, see:
http://www.cren.net:8080/guest/archives/AAHESGIT/ and
http://www.cren.net:8080/guest/archives/TLT-SWG/

Badley, G. & Marshall, S. (1995) *53 Questions and Answers about Modules and Semesters*. Bristol: TES

Bashir, T. (1994) Providing students with flexibility and choice. In Atrill, P., McLaney, E. & Gibbs, G. *Course Design for Resource Based Learning in Accountancy*. Oxford: Oxford Centre for Staff Development

Biggs, J. (1999) *Teaching for Quality Learning at University*. Buckingham: SRHE/Open University Press

Blackboard (2002) Available at url:
http://www.products.blackboard.com/index.cqi

Bryson, B. (1993) *Notes from a Small Island*. London: Doubleday

Court, S. (2002) 2010: A date with destiny. *Autlook* 22

Dawkins, R. (1999) The Observant Mind. Originally published in the *Daily Telegraph* quoted in *Oxford Today*

Ehrmann, S. (2000) Asking better questions about being there vs taming technology. AAHESGIT-65 15/11/00

Elsmore, M. (1999) Developing a student strategy for exam preparation. In Hinett K. & Thomas, J. *Staff Guide to Self and Peer Assessment.* Oxford: Oxford Centre for Staff and Learning Development

Gibbs, G. (1992) *Teaching More Students 4: Assessing More Students.* Oxford: Oxford Centre for Staff Development

Gibbs, G. (1994) *Course Design for Resource Based Learning: in Accountancy*, with Atrill,P., McLaney,E.; *in Art and Design*, with Wilkes, M.; *in Business*, with Eastcott, D., Farmer, B.; *in Built Environment*, with Brown, S.; *in Education*, with Parsons, C.; *in Social Science*, with Cox, C.; *in Science*, with Exley, K; *in Technology*, with Percival, F.; *in Humanities*, with Wisdom, J. Oxford: Oxford Centre for Staff Development

Gibbs, G., Pollard, N. & Farrell, J. (1995) *Institutional Support for Resource Based Learning.* Oxford: Oxford Centre for Staff Development

Gibbs, G. (1995a) *Assessing Student Centred Courses.* Oxford: Oxford Centre for Staff Development

Gibbs, G. (1995b) Peer assessment of engineering problems using marking schemes. With Forbes, D. & Spence, J. *Assessing Student Centred Courses.* Oxford: Oxford Centre for Staff Development

Gibbs, G. (1995c) Self and peer assessment on a counselling skills course. With Habeshaw, T. & Habeshaw, S. *Assessing Student Centred Courses.* Oxford: Oxford Centre for Staff Development

Gibbs, G. (1995d) *Learning in Teams: Tutor Guide.* Oxford: Oxford Centre for Staff Development

Gibbs, G., Habeshaw, S. & Habeshaw, T. (1988) *53 Interesting Ways to Improve Your Teaching.* Oxford: Oxford Centre for Staff and Learning Development

Goodlad, S. (1999) Benchmarks and templates – some notes and queries from a sceptic. In Smith, H., Armstrong, M. & Brown, S. *Benchmarking and Threshold Standards in Higher Education.* UK: SEDA, Kogan Page

Gosling, D. & Moon, J. (2001) *How to Use Learning Outcomes and Assessment Criteria.* London: Southern England Consortium for Credit Accumulation and Transfer (SEEC)

Grebenick, P. & Rust, C. (2002) IT to the rescue. In Schwartz, P. & Webb, G. (eds.) *Assessment Case Studies, Experience and Practice from Higher Education.* London: Kogan Page

Harvey, J. (1998) *Evaluation Cookbook.* Edinburgh: LTDI, Herriot-Watt University

Hinnett, K. & Thomas, J. (1999) *Staff Guide to Self and Peer Assessment.* Oxford: Oxford Centre for Staff and Learning Development

Hounsell, D., Tait, H. & Day, K. (1997) *Feedback on Courses and Programmes of Study.* Edinburgh: University of Edinburgh

Hurcombe, L., Bonsall, M. & Godfrey, J. (1995) *A University-wide View of S & M.* Sheffield: Teaching and Learning Development Group, University of Sheffield

InCAA (1998) Common Framework for Learning *Inter-Consortium Credit Agreement (InCAA),* DfEE and HEQE

Jackson, N. (1998a) Understanding standards-based quality assurance, part I – rationale and conceptual basis. *Quality Assurance in Education, 6.* MCB University Press

Jackson, N. (1998b) Understanding standards-based quality assurance, part II – nuts and bolts of the Dearing policy framework. *Quality Assurance in Education, 6.* MCB University Press

Jenkins, A. & Walker, L. (1994) *Developing Student Capability Through Modular Courses.* London: Kogan Page

Laming, D. (1990) The reliability of a certain university examination compared with the precision of absolute judgements. *Quarterly Journal of Experimental Psychology Section A– Human Experimental Psychology, 42, 2 239–254*

Lindsay, R., Paton-Saltzberg, R. & Turner, D.J. (1998) Some effects of programme structure on student marks. *Teaching Forum 46*

Marino, T. (2001) The art of teaching, AAHESGIT-92: 3/28/01

Maughan, C. & Moore, K. (1999) Peer-assessment: giving and receiving feedback on draft assignments. In Hinett, K. & Thomas, J. *Staff Guide to Self and Peer Assessment.* Oxford: Oxford Centre for Staff and Learning Development

Millis, B. (2001) Managing and motivating distance learning group activities, AAHESGIT-73, 3/1/01

NCIHE (1997) National Committee of Inquiry into Higher Education, Summary Report (the Dearing Report). Available at url: www.leeds.ac.uk/educol/ncihe/sumrep.htm

Price, M., O'Donovan, B. & Rust, C. (2001) Strategies to develop students' understanding of assessment criteria and processes.In *Improving Student Learning – 8 Improving Student Learning Strategically.* Oxford: Oxford Centre for Staff and Learning Development

QAA (1998), *Higher Quality* 4, p.11

QAA (1999a), Developing a programme file for HE, QAA Consultation Paper, September

QAA (2000) Code of Practice for the Assessment of Students. Available at url: http://www.qaa.ac.uk

QAA Guidelines (2001) Guidelines for preparing programme specifications. Available at url: http://www.qaa.ac.uk

QAA (2001a) *The Framework for Higher Education Qualifications in England, Wales and Northern Ireland.* Gloucester: The Quality Assurance Agency for Higher Education

QAA (2001b) Academic Standards Psychology, Draft for Consultation, July 2001

QAA (2001c) Academic Standards Physics, Astronomy and Astrophysics, Draft for Consultation, July 2001

QAA (2001d) Academic Standards Music, Draft for Consultation, July 2001

QAA (2001e) Quality Assurance in UK Higher Education: A Brief Guide. Available at url: http://www.qaa.ac.uk, July 2001.

RNIB (2001a) 'See it right' campaign. Available at url: http://www.rnib.org.uk/access/-

RNIB (2001b) http://www.rnib.org.uk/services/trans.htm

Index

SACWG (1997), Turner, D.J. & Woolf, H., Honours classifications: the need for transparency. *New Academic* 6 (3), 10–12

Staddon, C. (2000) UPDATE, No. 70, Nov. 2000, p. 4

Teaching News (1999), Spring, p. 1. Oxford: Oxford Centre for Staff and Learning Development

TLT-SWG See AAHESGIT

UPDATE (2000), 70, November, p. 4

UPDATE (2001), 76, November, p. 1

WAI (2001) W3C WAI standards. Available at url: http://www.ww3.org/WAI/

Watson, D., Brookes, J., Coghill, C., Lindsay, R. & Scurry, D. (1989) *Managing the Modular Course: Perspective from Oxford Polytechnic.* Buckingham: SRHE/Open University Press